Promised Joy, Promised Judgment

A Cry for the City

by

Mark Dingemans

Promised Joy, Promised Judgment
Copyright © 2004 by Mark Dingemans
ALL RIGHTS RESERVED

All Scripture references are from the New American Standard Bible, copyright © 1960, 1962, 1963, 1968, 1971, 1972, 1973, 1975, 1977, unless otherwise indicated. References marked The Book are from The Book, an edition of The Living Bible, copyright © 1971, 1976 by Tyndale House Publishers, Inc., Wheaton, Illinois. All emphasis used within Scripture references is the author's.

Published by:

McDougal Publishing
P.O. Box 3595
Hagerstown, MD 21742-3595
www.mcdougalpublishing.com

McDougal Publishing is a ministry of The McDougal Foundation, Inc., a Maryland nonprofit corporation dedicated to the spreading of the Gospel of the Lord Jesus Christ to as many people as possible in the shortest time possible.

ISBN 1-58158-071-1

Printed in the United States of America
For Worldwide Distribution

Contact the author at:
Mark Dingemans
P.O. Box 764206
Dallas, TX 75376-4206
www.kairosnewsletter.net

Acknowledgments

I want to say thanks to several people who've both encouraged and, at times, unknowingly influenced me in the writing of this book.

Floyd McClung: I've never met you, but you probably planted the seeds in my heart in the early 1980's when you spoke at a morning session at Christ for the Nations Institute, while I was a student there. You spoke of God's heart for cities…and I was scared to death. But it was during my two years there that God began to give me a heart for the lost right here in Dallas. Thank you for speaking into my life.

Dr. Don and Cheri Crum, who encouraged me in my writing of the *Kairos* newsletters: Don, you prophesied to me from a cell phone as you were returning from Mexico more than five years ago that the Holy Spirit would have me write books that would go throughout the world. This is the first fulfillment of that word. You also encouraged Michele and me when we walked the lonely Mordecai road and few understood our walk. Much of what I have written was during this Mordecai place.

Scott Hinkle of Scott Hinkle Outreach Ministries (SHOM): You continually and passionately keep alive the vision of God's desire for souls out of the megalopolises of our own land. It's easier to support and have a vision for faraway lands, but you and Nancy have walked the hard road here in the USA.

McDougal Publishing: Thank you so much for believing in the message of this book to publish it, even though I'm a nobody. Thank you so much for the encouragement to believe God four years ago for the finances to publish this book.

My wife, Michele, who first heard from the Holy Spirit concerning the difficult and lonely Mordecai walk we ventured into for our own city: Thank you so much for supporting me in the long, long hours and months of writing this book, and for encouraging me to get it published.

And finally, with every fiber of my being, I wish to thank the Holy Spirit, who poured out the passion of Jesus into Michele and me for the souls of our city and for the cities of nations. Lord Jesus, You continually met with us in our home with Your fragrance and Your glory when we needed the emotional support, when we wondered if we were still in the will of God. You also taught me as I wrote. May You receive fruit from this publication with the evidence of souls from the hardest of places.

Mark Dingemans
January 2004

Contents

Introduction 7

1. Promised Joy, Promised Judgment and a Cry for the City 13

2. Looking for the "Stand in the Gap" Man 33

3. Judgment: The Very First One… With Prophetic Hope 41

4. Who Is Judgment Ultimately For? God's Divine Intention 57

5. Justice and the Love of God: Is There a Conflict? 63

6. Longing for the Justice of God… and the Souls of Men 81

7. Desiring Judgment on the City Versus the Heart of God 89

8. A Cry for Unrighteous Leaders 101

9. Faith for Justice 115

10. For Such a Time as This: The Story of Esther 123

11. The Spirit and the Bride Say,
    "Come"…to Whom? 153

12. One Man, One Thousand Demons
    and One City…Meet Jesus 159

13. The Judge, the Accused
    and the Judging Accusers 167

14. The Seed of the Woman:
    Fulfilling the First Judgment 179

15. Justice From the Throne:
    The Role of the Holy Spirit 197

16. Distributing Plunder:
    Evidence of God's Justice and Judgment 209

17. The City of Tyre:
    The Standard on Judgment Day! 219

18. The Judgment Seat of Christ 235

19. The Final White Throne Judgment 243

20. A Cry for the City 253

INTRODUCTION

"Joy…judgment…and crying for cities? What's this all about?" you may ask.

I know it sounds strange, so let me satisfy your curiosity. This book is the result of laughter, and of crying, during a move of God that swept a number of nations in the early to mid 1990's.

This book is also a prophetic look at God's purposes—indeed, God's very heart—for bringing His Church to a strategic place before Him and before the world so as to rightly respond to future events. I will clearly state that there are hard issues concerning judgment in this book; these will change your entire perspective on both God and people who have no faith in Jesus or fear of God whatsoever. You will not finish this book indifferent to the subject of judgment.

For those of you who were intimately acquainted with the renewal, you will see the renewal of the 1990's as more than just a move of God in history. You will see clearly that, as other moves of God in the past, it was an integral part of God's plan—a building block, if you will—toward the completion and consummation of something greater than just a move of God in a moment of time. You will discover it to be a climactic event in the history of creation.

My own discovery of the meaning of these events starts here….

Dallas, Texas, in the summer of 1980 was hot. It seemed brown and ugly. There, I was a student at Christ for the Nations Institute for two years. My goal was to live in a rural area while preaching the Gospel in the city. I had lived in the city of Scarborough, Ontario, as a small child, but my family had moved to the countryside when I was about eight or nine years old. I was not comfortable with city living.

One day a guest speaker had come to the Institute from Youth With A Mission in Amsterdam, Holland. He spoke about God's heart for the cities. I heard him…and trembled. I had no burden for any city. After all, cities were infested with crime, drugs and every evil thing. Why would any Christian want to live in a city? But his message became a dormant seed in my heart.

After graduating from CFNI, I went to Bolivia, South America. There I served as a teacher to deaf children for seven months in the town of Vinto. The area, though poor, was beautiful rural countryside. It suited me.

After my term of service, I married Michele Cowan, a fellow graduate of CFNI. We settled in the Dallas area—in the suburbs. I started a landscape and irrigation business and we did just fine until 1993. Two large contracts went awry, causing the business to flounder. Within a year I was forced to shut it down. I did not realize that God was about to use these circumstances to change my heart for His purposes.

Then Michele and I attended a prayer meeting at the home of some friends. During the meeting, we heard a message concerning Jesus' passion to return for His Bride.

About two weeks later, an outpouring of God's Holy Spirit began at Oak Cliff Assembly of God Church in south Dallas. (This was about the same time as the outpouring of the Holy Spirit which began at the Airport Vineyard Church near Toronto, Ontario.) We were drawn there for those meetings by our hunger. During that two-week revival, the supernatural joy of the Holy Spirit was poured out on many people. We saw whole families come to believe on the Lord Jesus during those days.

After two weeks, it seemed as if the Spirit of God lifted from within the highway loop of Dallas, and moved outside of that loop. Meetings were then held at Church on the Rock in Rockwall, a small city to the east of Dallas. For six weeks people flocked to this church building as the Holy Spirit poured out in joy and weeping. More than 700 people were baptized after just the first two weeks. My wife and I went to these meetings like a dying couple in desperate need of sustenance.

Throughout that year I wept continually. My heart began to be stirred for the souls of nations. As I watched God touch people with such joy that they would run to the altar for salvation, I cried before the Lord, telling Him that I wanted to take this outpouring to the nations of the world. I didn't realize that God was working in both my wife's and my heart to desire His will and to see Him pour out His Spirit here in this nation and in the very city we were about to leave!

In January 1995, a lightning bolt of God's Holy Spirit struck me to the floor with laughter. I would laugh for the next twelve months. At the least expected times throughout that year, I would burst out laughing. No one could convince me that this was not from God's Holy Spirit. I had been as skeptical as any concerning this "holy laughter." But God hit me with His laughter anyway, and I learned that I had been wrong about it.

During that year, my wife and I had a noticeable change of heart toward the city in which we dwelt. By mid-summer, all Michele and I could do was talk about and pray about our own city. We had a growing passion to see God's salvation come to Dallas. Our hearts were stirred as we watched the news and saw reports of the crime and violence within the loop. We also ached as we realized that the move of God within the local churches was hardly producing any compassion for the city of Dallas.

It was at this time that God put it into our hearts to leave the church we were attending…and not join any other church. I can hear some saying, *"God wouldn't do that. The Bible says not to forsake the assembling of the saints. God wouldn't lead you out if He wasn't going to lead you in somewhere else."*

But He did! Did we feel the criticisms? Absolutely! But God showed us that we did not have to keep defending our position to try to maintain a good image. We did not walk perfectly in His peace—we wanted so much for our brothers and sisters in the Lord to understand what the Lord was doing in and through us. Though we could explain scripturally what God was doing, many others did not really hear what we were saying. However, I will explain here, because in this story lies the basis for understanding this book.

As the renewal of 1994 came, especially through the Toronto Airport Vineyard Church and around the Dallas area, the Holy Spirit began to clearly show Michele and me the correlation of this outpouring to the story of Esther in the Bible.

The Church, before this outpouring, had been like the first wife of King Ahasuerus; she was Queen Vashti, full of pride, not submissive to her husband the king. We saw how Jesus, in renewal, was drawing to Himself a new Bride. Esther, the renewal Church, first had to come to His house and soak in His fragrances. The Church had a calling to the lost, but she smelled too much like the world and looked too much like the world. It was time to be brought into the house of the King to soak in His fragrances, in His oils of the Holy Spirit, so that He could choose her as a beautiful Bride *"for such a time as this."*

Like Esther, who was chosen and who went on to remain in the king's palace apart from the world, my wife and I saw how the renewal Church remained inside the palace. During this season of renewal, my wife spent the evening hours seeking God in prayer. He allowed her to hear the cry of the lost in the city. God then had us move inside the city loop to sit among the lost, even as He had moved Mordecai out of the palace to sit among those who had been condemned to die (see Esther 4:1-2).

For two years God did not allow us to join any church, no matter how powerfully the Holy Spirit was pouring upon them. We were to stay out with the lost and feel their Sunday aloneness. And, as Mordecai pleaded with Esther to understand Haman's decree of judgment, my wife and I tried to make believers hear and understand the cry of the lost in our city. But, just as Esther had tried to bring Mordecai back into the palace with new clothes, fellow believers who did not hear the cries of the lost tried to convince us to attend church again and again. We were amazed that after sitting in such abundance, the renewal Church had no feeling or motivation to serve the lost, but only to stay where they could continually soak, untouched by the afflictions of the lost.

The promised joy was poured out around Dallas and throughout parts of the world around — but not always in—major cities. The renewal in Toronto at the Airport Vineyard Church had actually begun outside of Toronto—in a suburb. A similar move of God in Mexico had, as in Dallas, started inside a certain city, but then moved outside of that city for a year. However, after that time it was back inside the city. God's desire is the core of big cities. Cities are the hardest ground; yet, like Jericho of old, the harder they are to penetrate, the greater the glory to God when the walls come down.

Let me mention one more point from the book of Esther. At the end of chapter three, it is written that there was drinking in the palace and confusion in the city streets. Esther was little moved for her city. She would have to be persuaded...or else a judgment would overtake her city, and the decree of death would be carried out. Her heart had to be changed from "I really am not moved for the city" to a place of putting her life in danger—for her city and for those doomed to death in so many cities within her husband's empire. Indifference toward judgment is the same as desiring it. Judgment is not the desire of the King of kings. It is the desire of some of His people. Yet the King is sitting in His throne room...waiting to see if His Bride will put her life on the line in intercession for cities, for nations.

This book is written from a Mordecai perspective of judgment with the prayer that God will cause you to see and understand His view of judgment, and give you, the Bride of Christ, a desire to cry out to Him for cities.

May God impart to you some of the deep-hearted feelings of Mordecai. For presently there are those who have against them a decreed judgment of death waiting to be carried out....

Unless you are moved....

Mark Dingemans
Dallas, Texas

One

Promised Joy, Promised Judgment and a Cry for the City

For years the Church has been hearing about a great end-time harvest of souls. And for years we have heard of the judgments to come, as spoken of in the book of Revelation. We have been excited about the former and scared stiff about the latter. The end result, at least in the North American Church, has been a confused cry: "Jesus, hurry up and get back here to get me out of this mess down here!" We want no part of the judgments to come. None of us wants to be here when every sort of chaos hits the earth.

But…what if God Himself came to visit you and told you that He was about to destroy the city just over the hill from where you live? How would you respond? Would you hurry to pack so you could get your family away from there?

I know of a family like that. They are certain that God is "fixin' to judge the U.S." in a major way. They live in one of the suburbs of Dallas; but they can't wait to move to the countryside of another state and "let God start judgin'; after all, the city is so full of sin." This attitude is understandable in some ways—who can argue that there is sin in our nation? But should this be the attitude of the godly?

Abraham had a different kind of response. Genesis chapter 18 shows his reaction to divine judgment about to be poured out upon the unrighteous.

> *Now the L*ORD *appeared to him* [Abraham] *by the oaks of Mamre, while he was sitting at the tent door in the heat of the day. And when he lifted up his eyes and looked, behold, three men were standing opposite him; and when he saw them, he ran from the tent door to meet them, and bowed himself to the earth, and said, "My lord, if now I have found favor in your sight, please do not pass your servant by. Please let a little water be brought and wash your feet, and rest yourselves under the tree; and I will bring a piece of bread, that you may refresh yourselves; after that you may go on since you have visited your servant."*
>
> *And they said, "So do, as you have said."*
>
> *So Abraham hurried into the tent to Sarah, and said, "Quickly, prepare three measures of fine flour, knead it, and make bread cakes." Abraham also ran to the herd, and took a tender and choice calf, and gave it to the servant; and he hurried to prepare it. And he took curds and milk and the calf which he had prepared, and placed it before them; and he was standing by them under the tree as they ate.*

> *Then they said to him, "Where is Sarah your wife?"*
>
> *And he said, "Behold, in the tent."*
>
> *And he said, "I will surely return to you at this time next year; and behold, Sarah your wife shall have a son."*
>
> *And Sarah was listening at the tent door, which was behind him. Now Abraham and Sarah were old, advanced in age; Sarah was past childbearing. And Sarah laughed to herself, saying, "After I have become old, shall I have pleasure, my lord being old also?"*
>
> *And the L*ORD *said to Abraham, "Why did Sarah laugh, saying, 'Shall I indeed bear a child, when I am so old?' "Is anything too difficult for the L*ORD*? At the appointed time I will return to you, at this time next year, and Sarah will have a son."*
>
> *Sarah denied it however, saying, "I did not laugh"; for she was afraid.*
>
> *And He said, "No, but you did laugh."*
>
> Genesis 18:1-15

In Genesis 17, Abraham had received a name change from his birth name of Abram. The time frame between chapters 17 and 18 is extremely close, possibly within the same month; for in both chapters, God tells Abraham that He will return the next year to give him and Sarah a son. In chapter 17, Abraham laughs when God tells him this news. In chapter 18, Sarah laughs. And so they were to have a son named "Isaac," which means "laughter."

At this point in their lives, this elderly couple was not able to conceive children. God had waited until it was entirely beyond their power. Their dream of passing on the family name was dead by all appearances (see Romans 4:19, Hebrews 11:11-12). Abraham had been given the promise of being the father, through Sarah, of many nations, but in the natural it seemed impossible. Instead, the couple had tried to fulfill that promise in their own strength by having a surrogate son, Ishmael, through Sarah's maid Hagar. But God reaffirmed His promise, clearly stating that He would establish His covenant through Sarah's son and not through Ishmael. The couple's attempts to bring the promise to pass in their own strength were futile efforts.

We can easily see the parallels of this situation with the Church today. We have clung to the prophetic words concerning a great end-time harvest. This would be fine if we were looking to the Lord to fulfill this prophecy. Unfortunately, the Church is desperately trying everything in her own ability to birth the lost into the Kingdom of God. Our testimony has become, "Not by faith, but by works, so that we may have something to boast about before God and before everyone else."

It doesn't look good, in a world that demands quick results, to say that we have no ability within ourselves to accomplish the work of God. The problem, however, is that we have birthed competition and division as we try with every ounce of strength within to make "our" churches bigger instead of caring for the growth of Jesus' Church. And so we kick and bite and mock, growing jealous of our very brothers and sisters in the Lord when we see them doing things better—or even differently—than we do. You see, Ishmael always mocks what is birthed of God's Spirit (see Genesis 21:9, Galatians 4:29).

Promised Joy, Promised Judgment and a Cry for the City

This became evident to me during the outpouring of God at the Airport Vineyard in Toronto. Another church in that city, one with which I am familiar, refused to go to the Vineyard: It was not their church. Initially, they disparaged what God was doing across town. Other people were traveling from the nations of the earth to jump into this river of life that was flowing so close to them. Yet when I pleaded with an acquaintance who attends that church to go and participate in what God was doing at the Vineyard, the person refused to go. What was taking place across town was not part of her denomination, and she would not participate in it. Ishmael was mocking Isaac.

Back to our story in Genesis 18:

> *Then the men rose up from there, and looked down toward Sodom; and Abraham was walking with them to send them off. And the LORD said, "Shall I hide from Abraham what I am about to do, since Abraham will surely become a great and mighty nation, and in him all the nations of the earth will be blessed? For I have chosen him, in order that he may command his children and his household after him to keep the way of the LORD by doing righteousness and justice; in order that the LORD may bring upon Abraham what He has spoken about him."*
>
> *And the LORD said, "The outcry of Sodom and Gomorrah is indeed great, and their sin is exceedingly grave. I will go down now, and see if they have done entirely according to its outcry, which has come to Me; and if not, I will know."*
>
> *Then the men turned away from there and*

went toward Sodom, while Abraham was still standing before the LORD.

And Abraham came near and said, "Wilt Thou indeed sweep away the righteous with the wicked? Suppose there are fifty righteous within the city; wilt Thou indeed sweep it away and not spare the place for the sake of the fifty righteous who are in it? Far be it from Thee to do such a thing, to slay the righteous with the wicked, so that the righteous and the wicked are treated alike. Far be it from Thee! Shall not the Judge of all the earth deal justly?"

So the LORD *said, "If I find in Sodom fifty righteous within the city, then I will spare the whole place on their account."*

And Abraham answered and said, "Now behold, I have ventured to speak to the Lord, although I am but dust and ashes. Suppose the fifty righteous are lacking five, wilt Thou destroy the whole city because of five?"

And He said, "I will not destroy it if I find forty-five there."

And he spoke to Him yet again and said, "Suppose forty are found there?"

And He said, "I will not do it on account of the forty."

Then he said, "Oh may the Lord not be angry, and I shall speak; suppose thirty are found there?"

And He said, "I will not do it if I find thirty there."

And he said, "Now behold, I have ventured to speak to the Lord; suppose twenty are found there?"

And He said, "I will not destroy it on account

of the twenty."

Then he said, "Oh may the Lord not be angry, and I shall speak only this once; suppose ten are found there?

*And He said, "I will not destroy it on account of the ten." And as soon as He had finished speaking to Abraham the L*ORD *departed; and Abraham returned to his place.*   Genesis 18: 16-33

It's not happenstance or coincidence that two seemingly different issues are being discussed here, that is, that God has promised to give this old couple joy through the promised birth of a son, and also that God is going to judge a nearby city. It is too easy to read the chapter as such. But with God, these two things are *joint issues.* There is a divine purpose in God's heart for bringing up both the promise of joy and the promise of judgment at the same time.

If you look back at chapter 17, you will notice that when God tells Abraham he will be a father within one year, He also changes his name from his given name, Abram, to a new name, Abraham. I believe it is significant that this name change occurs around the same time that God reveals His intended judgment on Sodom. The name *Abraham* means "father of a multitude." God's covenant promise to Abraham was *"And you shall be a father of a multitude of nations"* (Genesis 17:4b). It is important that we understand the word *"nations"* in the Old Testament context if we are to understand the quality of righteousness that Abraham displayed, enabling him to pray as he did for the wicked city over the hill from his camp.

Look again at God's words regarding His intention

concerning Sodom and Gomorrah.

> *And the LORD said, "Shall I hide from Abraham what I am about to do, since Abraham will surely become a great and mighty NATION, and in Him all the nations of the earth will be blessed? For I have chosen him, in order that he may command his children and his household after him to keep the way of the LORD by doing righteousness and justice; in order that the LORD may bring upon Abraham what He has spoken about him."*
>
> Genesis 18:17-19

Now, in Genesis 18, we find that God was about to tell this one who would become a nation through his promised child, Laughter, what He planned to do with the cities over the hill from Abraham's camp. He spoke of the character of the nation that would eventually descend from Abraham, a nation of righteousness and justice—in other words, the complete opposite character from that of the cities He was about to destroy.

The Hebrew definition for the word *nation* denotes "a mass or confluence of people." Thus, nations were people groups known by their cities! We see one example of this in the wording of a passage in Deuteronomy:

> *"Thus you shall do to all the cities that are very far from you, which are not of the CITIES OF THESE NATIONS nearby."*
>
> Deuteronomy 20:15

And look at this passage from the book of Joshua:

Promised Joy, Promised Judgment and a Cry for the City

Now these are the kings of the land whom Joshua and the sons of Israel defeated beyond the Jordan toward the west...the Hittite, the Amorite and the Canaanite, the Perizzite, the Hivite and the Jebusite: the king of Jericho, one; the king of Ai, which is beside Bethel, one; the king of Jerusalem, one; the king of Hebron, one; the king of Jarmuth, one; the king of Lachish, one; the king of Eglon, one; the king of Gezer, one; the king of Debir, one; the king of Geder, one; the king of Hormah, one; the king of Arad, one; the king of Libnah, one; the king of Adullam, one; the king of Makkedah, one; the king of Bethel, one; the king of Tappuah, one; the king of Hepher, one; the king of Aphek, one; the king of Lasharon, one; the king of Madon, one; the king of Hazor, one; the king of Shimron-meron, one; the king of Achshaph, one; the king of Taanach, one; the king of Megiddo, one; the king of Kedesh, one; the king of Jokneam in Carmel, one; the king of Dor in the heights of Dor, one; the king of Goiim in Gilgal, one; the king of Tirzah, one: in all, thirty-one kings. Joshua 12:7a, 8b-24

Does this list seem monotonous to you? Did you read all of the names? Each of these was a king over a city. These cities made up the *nations* which Joshua had defeated. If you look at the second to last king mentioned, you will see the phrase "*the king of Goiim in Gilgal.*" The King James Version of the Bible gives the translation of *Goiim* in that verse: "*the king of THE NATIONS of Gilgal.*" The king of that city was actually a king over nations. Nations were made up of cities. Cities were made up of families. (See Genesis 10:31.)

And so, we come to the initial promise by God to Abraham in Genesis chapter 12:

> *Now the LORD said to Abram, "Go forth from your country, and from your relatives and from your father's house, to the land which I will show you; and I will make you a great nation, and I will bless you, and make your name great; and so you shall be a blessing; and I will bless those who bless you, and the one who curses you I will curse. And in you all the families of the earth shall be blessed."*
>
> Genesis 12:1-3

God told Abram to leave his nation, his relatives and his father's house. Why? So that God Himself could make of Abraham a new father, family and nation. We don't say that Abram left Chaldea, but that he left Ur of the Chaldeans (Genesis 11:31). When he left his city, he left his nation. Abram would become a new kind of family, a new kind of nation, having a new kind of character, with a new name.

But this change of name, with the promised joy of a new son, *is in direct conjunction with the promised judgment of a city-nation,* and the intercession that would follow for that city-nation. These are not separate incidents; they are entirely interwoven.

And so we read of the situation of the cities of Sodom and Gomorrah in Genesis 18. Before God revealed what He was about to do with these wicked cities, He revealed Himself to Abraham twice (see Genesis 17 and 18) to promise him laughter and a heritage. Again, we know that God waited until Abraham had absolutely no ability to fulfill the promise. I do not say that Abraham had no faith; his faith was strong (see Romans 4:19-21). His faith loudly shouted, "God is able to bring life from the dead!" Thus, in the midst of barrenness comes the promise of laughter.

I believe this is the place in which the Church now finds herself. We are coming to the end of ourselves in realizing that we are unable to fulfill the Great Commission, that is, the birthing of *"a multitude of nations"* into the Kingdom of God. We must see our barrenness—actually look at it and comprehend our own complete inability to do anything about it—and then declare God's ability through the work of His Son Jesus:

> *...for Thou wast slain, and didst purchase for God with Thy blood men from every tribe and tongue and people and nation.*
> Revelation 5:9b

There can be no boasting on our part, else we birth Ishmaels. But when we acknowledge our need for God's power to work in and through us, we receive a promise of joy as did Abraham, our father of faith:

> *"Shout for joy, O barren one, you who have borne no child; break forth into joyful shouting and cry aloud, you who have not travailed; for the sons of the desolate one will be more numerous than the sons of the married woman," says the LORD.*
> Isaiah 54:1

The laughter that has come to the Church is the promise of God that the barrenness of the Church, the Bride of Christ, is about to be broken. And a change of name, even as Abram was transformed into Abraham, is coming also. We are in a time of transition.

One of the poignant aspects of this account in Genesis 18 is that although there was such joy at the promise of the heir to come, the promise of judgment upon the nearby peoples followed almost immediately. Abraham was somewhat removed from the people of Sodom geographically. Yes, he was kin to one person in that doomed city-nation area—his nephew Lot lived in Sodom.

Yet there is something even more significant to this story than the one relative Abraham knew there in Sodom, something of substantial importance which had taken place years before this present situation, something that would move Abraham to intercede, not only for his nephew, but for the cities themselves.

Abraham was ninety-nine years old when God came with the promise of the child (see Genesis 17:1). It had been thirteen years earlier, while he was still called Abram, that Ishmael was born (see Genesis 16:16). Sometime prior to that, Abram's nephew Lot had moved away from him to live in the area of Sodom, a valley lush with vegetation. Lot knew that his livestock would do well there (see Genesis 13:6-11).

During the days of Lot's dwelling in and around Sodom, the city was under the rulership of a mightier city-nation, with King Chedorlaomer (*ke-door-la-o-mer*) as its ruler (see Genesis 14). Sodom's king, along with four other local kings of the southern Dead Sea area, rebelled against the rulership of Chedorlaomer, which brought the wrath of Chedorlaomer and three of his allies against them. The four kings of the east traveled the great distance from their homeland, and soundly defeated the five kings of the Dead Sea area. The result of the battle for those who lived was exile.

Chedorlaomer's army was transporting the survivors back to his homeland as slaves. But one Sodomite escaped and ran for a point northwest: Abram's camp. He told Abram of the battle and its outcome. As the old man listened, he realized that he personally knew one man among all the exiles being taken away. Lot and his family were being hauled like cattle northward, and then they would be taken several hundred miles east.

The old man, then in his late seventies or early eighties, acted quickly. He mustered a small army of 318 men of those born in his own household, along with three Amorite brothers and their men, and pursued the four mighty kings. They quickly overtook Chedorlaomer's army north of Damascus and defeated them. They set Lot and his family free…and then they freed the wicked people of the Sodom and Gomorrah valley region.

Abram could have freed only his relative. However, he risked his life for all the people of the immoral cities of the Dead Sea valley, and he brought them back safely. Is it possible that Abram, this righteous man who most likely raised Lot, the son of his dead brother (see Genesis 11:27-28, 12:4), hoped that the righteous characteristics of Lot would move some people within Sodom to change their evil ways? (We know that Lot himself was righteous because the Scriptures tell us this in 2 Peter 2:7.)

I must admit that for years I believed Lot was downright foolish to move his family into Sodom. Yet as I have studied Genesis, I have come to believe that Lot did not simply close his eyes to the filth of the sin around him. I believe he did love the greenness of the valley for his livestock. Perhaps because of this he hoped to change the moral climate of the city. Maybe he saw the potential of the entire area. I believe Lot really desired to see change for righteousness. Perhaps this was a godly characteristic learned from growing up under his uncle's guidance.

As we return to the events of Genesis 19, we find two of Abraham's three visitors walking into Sodom. These two angels had left the Lord and Abraham as they talked together about the coming judgment, and had walked on ahead to the city. Remember, this is at least fourteen or fifteen years after the city had been rescued by Abram from the clutches of Chedorlaomer. And the angels came to the city with only one possible hope: They were looking for just ten righteous people within the city so that they could spare it.

> *Now the two angels came to Sodom in the evening AS LOT WAS SITTING IN THE GATE OF SODOM. When Lot saw them, he rose to meet them and bowed down with his face to the ground.*   Genesis 19:1

Lot was sitting in the gate. This tells us that he was making an effort to bring some form of righteousness and justice to the city, for the gates of the cities were the seat of government in the Old Testament.

> *"This one came in as an alien, and already he is acting like a judge...."*   Genesis 19:9

Lot hated what he saw taking place around him on a daily basis (see 2 Peter 2:8). He wanted a change to take place for good in his city. Again we recall what God had said concerning Abraham:

> *"For I have chosen him, IN ORDER THAT HE MAY COMMAND HIS CHILDREN AND HIS HOUSEHOLD AFTER HIM TO KEEP THE WAY OF THE LORD BY DOING RIGHTEOUSNESS AND JUSTICE; in order that the LORD may bring upon Abraham what He has spoken about him."*
> Genesis 18:19

Abraham had brought up Lot as his own child. Now Lot was walking in the ways his adoptive father had taught him. I believe he also held hope by faith for the people of his city: Had he given up on them, he would have long since moved out of Sodom.

But despite Lot's desire and his efforts, a change for righteousness was not taking place in his adopted city.

> *Now the two angels came to Sodom in the evening as Lot was sitting in the gate of Sodom. When Lot saw them, he rose to meet them and bowed down with his face to the ground.*
>
> *And he said, "Now behold, my lords, please turn aside into your servant's house, and spend the night, and wash your feet; then you may rise early and go on your way."*
>
> *They said however, "No, but we shall spend the night in the square."*
>
> *Yet he urged them strongly, so they turned aside to him and entered his house; and he prepared a feast for them, and baked unleavened bread, and they ate.*
> Genesis 19:1-3

Promised Joy, Promised Judgment

Lot did not know that these two strangers were angels. He simply thought them guests from a place other than the Jordan valley area. He was not willing for them to stay in the city square because of the danger to them from the wickedness of the people.

> *Before they lay down, the men of the city, the men of Sodom, surrounded the house, both young and old, all the people from every quarter; and they called to Lot and said to him, "Where are the men who came to you tonight? Bring them out to us that we may have relations with them."*
>
> *But Lot went out to them at the doorway, and shut the door behind him, and said, "Please, my brothers, do not act wickedly."...*
>
> *But they said, "Stand aside." Furthermore, they said, "This one came in as an alien, and already he is acting like a judge; now we will treat you worse than them." So they pressed hard against Lot and came near to break the door.*
>
> Genesis 19:4-7, 9

Lot begged the men not to harm his guests. But his pleas fell upon deaf ears, as the men of Sodom were single-minded in pursuing their objective. The angels within Lot's house quickly reached out their hands and jerked him back inside. Then they struck the men outside with blindness. Lot suddenly realized that these guests were not merely strangers passing through the region, but that they had come to the city on a divine mission.

The supernatural God, who had made Himself

known several times to his uncle, was now making Himself known directly to Lot. Abraham's nephew was now face-to-face with the supernatural power of God. And Lot's heart was pounding. These guests, who had just finished feasting with Lot's family, were now hurrying to get that family out of the Jordan valley's south end. Their purpose was to come to *"see if they* [Sodom] *have done entirely according to its outcry"* which had risen up to God in Heaven (see Genesis 18:21). The answer was sickeningly obvious. Lot's efforts to somehow bring a righteous change within the valley area had borne no fruit.

But desperation within Lot's heart for the souls of Sodom cried out in frenzied action in the final hours before judgment poured out from the heavens.

> *Then the men* [the visiting angels] *said to Lot, "Whom else have you here? A son-in-law, and your sons, and your daughters, and whomever you have in the city, bring them out of the place; for we are about to destroy this place, because their outcry has become so great before the* LORD *that the* LORD *has sent us to destroy it."*
>
> *And Lot went out and spoke to his sons-in-law, who were to marry his daughters, and said, "UP, GET OUT OF THIS PLACE, FOR THE LORD WILL DESTROY THE CITY." But he appeared to his sons-in-law to be jesting.*
>
> Genesis 19:12-14

Both the mercy shown by Abraham and the righteous and just example of Lot were rejected by the people of the city. Consequently, this stench of rejected mercy, along with pride and years of blatant sin, had piled up as high as Heaven—all the way to the throne of God. This stink of sin moved God to come to earth, showing that He was seeking to be able to give mercy even still to the sinners. (The ever-increasing sin of the world would move Him again to return to earth several millennia later to render mercy for all in every city ever built.)

Yet even though the sin of the southern Dead Sea valley region rose to Heaven and tormented the soul of Lot, *it did not move Lot to cry for judgment! It also did not bring a cry for judgment from Abraham*, who had just spoken with the holy Lord. And I do not believe God Himself was moved to "see the sinners fried." I'm sorry for phrasing it this way, but I believe this attitude exists in some Christians. If God was moved by a desire for annihilation, He would not first have brought up the situation with Abraham. God, who knows all things, knew what Abraham would do. He knew that this man, whom He had called to bless all the nations of the earth, *would stand in the gap* for this city-nation which he himself had saved years earlier!

Beloved, please hear this. Abraham had only one relative in Sodom. Nonetheless, he had looked into the eyes of the people of the valley region years before. And these people, with whom he had personally been involved, were about to be condemned in a severe judgment.

Before you seek God's judgment on a wicked people, go to their part of the city and walk its streets. Look into their empty eyes for a while. You cannot contain the compassion of God and still cry for judgment. If you do, I do not think you will have the ear of the Almighty, and I would question whether you have ever experienced His mercy in your own life.

Observe the heart of Lot on the morning of his city's judgment:

> *When morning dawned, the angels urged Lot, saying, "Up, take your wife and your two daughters, who are here, lest you be swept away in the punishment of the city." BUT HE HESITATED. So the men seized his hand and the hand of his wife and the hands of his daughters, FOR THE COMPASSION OF THE LORD WAS UPON HIM.*
> Genesis 19:15-16a

Compassion had moved God to come to the earth to seek an intercessor. He was looking for one who would stand in the gap to cry out for a city whose people reveled in their own wickedness. These people had absolutely no desire to reach heavenward for change themselves.

Compassion had moved an old man who had a call to bless the nations through righteousness and justice, even after he had received wonderful news of a personal promise of joy, to intercede for that wicked city.

And compassion had moved a younger man, who had been brought up in righteousness and justice, to delay leaving that wicked city; for he knew that once judgment began to be poured out onto the city, it would be lost for all eternity.

Abraham was a man of justice and compassion. He was a man who would father a multitude of a different character than that of the world around him. And all who would come into like faith—for justice and for compassion—would likewise receive a change of name.

They would be called Abraham's seed!

Two

Looking for the "Stand in the Gap" Man

And then He called to the man clothed in linen at whose loins was the writing case. And the LORD said to him, "GO THROUGH THE MIDST OF THE CITY, even through the midst of Jerusalem, AND PUT A MARK ON THE FOREHEADS OF THE MEN WHO SIGH AND GROAN OVER ALL THE ABOMINATIONS WHICH ARE BEING COMMITTED IN ITS MIDST."

Ezekiel 9:3b-4

At the end of 1997, I took a job delivering the new 1998 yellow pages for the phone company. We delivery people would pick routes and then deliver the prescribed number of books on those routes. There were usually only a few streets per route, depending on the number of buildings on each street. At the very end of our district's distribution, a different office in another area of the city suddenly closed without finishing their district distribution. Our office picked up the remainder of those routes. I chose a route in that district without first considering the exact location of the streets.

When I opened the map book to find that particular location, I realized with sudden shock just which part of the city I had selected. It was an area known historically for its prostitution, but in more recent times it had become the center of a very extensive homosexual community. One of the streets on my route was the commercial center for every homosexual bar, book and video store in the area, as well as for explicit clothing stores.

My first reaction was swift...I rejected the route.

Then suddenly my heart changed toward these people...by God's Spirit? I believe so. For my next thoughts were, *"If I don't go there and pray as I walk my route, nobody else will either."* It would have been too easy to simply wash my hands of that neighborhood and pick another route.

And so I took the route, delivering telephone books in shops I had not even dreamed existed in our city. At that time, I was somewhat naïve. I had been brought up in a very good home, with parents who loved me and who guarded my brother, sister and me from much knowledge of worldly and wicked lifestyles. And I had believed in Jesus as a young teenager.

Consequently, even though I knew this lifestyle existed, I had never really seen it with my own eyes. What I saw was more than strange to me. I had shared the Gospel over a week's period at Mardi Gras in New Orleans years before, and so I knew of this lifestyle, but I had not seen it to the extent I now found in my own city. As I delivered the phone books, my heart broke for the men and women caught up in this way of life. The

Lord used that day to change my attitude toward the homosexual community. I began to pray *for* these people, rather than *against* them.

After that time, the Holy Spirit would put it on my heart to return to that street just to walk and pray. I would go to church on Sundays and weep and weep for the homosexuals, while my heart would break and groan concerning their sin. God began to speak to me concerning His vision and heart for that whole area. From that time onward, I couldn't even listen to other men of God speak about the homosexuals because I had walked the streets; I had entered the bars and stores of this community. I had looked into the eyes of the men bound (even though they don't think they're in bondage) in this unnatural and perverted lust. I ached and prayed and longed for them to be set free to the abundance of the Kingdom of God.

I could no longer, from a distance, call for God to "judge these brash sinners." I know that one day there will be a judgment against all who continue in any form of sexual perversion and who do not turn to God. But vengeance and judgment belong to God. Prayers and passion for God's mercy belong to us. God's longing is for the latter to be accomplished before judgment becomes the only choice.

God is continually looking for, and taking note of, those who pray, those who stand in the gap between the wickedness of their cities and the deserved wrath of God. God is seeking those men and women and children who will stand in the breaches of the broken-down walls around their metropolises.

"The people of the land have practiced oppression

and committed robbery, and they have wronged the poor and needy and have oppressed the sojourner without justice. And I searched for a man among them who should build up the wall and stand in the gap before Me for the land, that I should not destroy it...."

Ezekiel 22:29-30

Those who will stand in the gap for their cities do not have to be known publicly. Their sighs and groans get the attention of the only One who needs to hear, the only One who is able to bring righteousness and justice to a city.

The nightly news attests to the fact that oppression and robbery are daily occurrences within our cities. The wrong done to the poor and needy is not always made known. But God sees it all (see Proverbs 15:3). And because this earth is His, and because His character demands justice for every evil committed—whether that evil is seen or unseen—judgment must be executed. Again I say that this God of justice earnestly longs to show mercy; He does not desire the death of the wicked, who will perish for all eternity.

This desire in God for mercy, however, does not mean that judgment for crime will not be carried out. Indeed, He would not be a true God of justice if He were to ignore sin. But this just God of righteousness *and* mercy has made a provision for wrongs *to be paid*. His mercy is based upon *His own provision* to satisfy the need for justice! Again, this does not mean that the penalty for crime is ignored. There will be those who will have to pay the consequences for their wrongdoing because of society's judicial requirements, even when they are completely made clean by the Blood of Jesus. But the cycle of sin will have been broken. In some cases this will also mean that the cycle of crime in a city is broken.

God is looking for those who will groan and sigh over sin, even as He does, to gain His mercy for those who need it. He is looking for a man who will stand in the gap so that He should not destroy cities according to their deserved punishment, if it is not too late. Remember Abraham and Sodom? How about Jonah and Nineveh?

What is being said is this: The "stand in the gap" man is the one who literally will stand between the condemned and the judgment to be poured out. A dangerous place? Perhaps. Look at a man who did stand in that place.

Numbers chapter 16 contains the account of the Lord's dealing with the sons of Israel at the time of a rebellion started by a man named Korah. Korah, of the same tribe as Moses, had stirred up other Levites against the authority of Moses and Aaron because he wanted equal authority. But the Lord, who had chosen Moses and Aaron, became angry with Korah and his followers because of their rebellion. That entire group fell under judgment and perished, along with their families.

The next day, the sons of Israel were angry with Moses and Aaron because of this. They charged them with having caused the death of the Lord's people. But something was happening as the people were accusing Moses and Aaron:

> *It came about, however, when the congregation had assembled against Moses and Aaron, that they turned toward the tent of meeting, and behold, the cloud covered it and the glory of the LORD*

appeared. Then Moses and Aaron came to the front of the tent of meeting, and the LORD spoke to Moses, saying, "Get away from among this congregation, that I may consume them instantly." Then they fell on their faces.

Numbers 16:42-45

The people did not realize that their challenge was not against Moses and Aaron, but against God Himself. Judgment from the Lord began to be poured out.

And Moses said to Aaron, "Take your censer and put in it fire from the altar, and lay incense on it; then bring it quickly to the congregation and make atonement for them, for wrath has gone forth from the LORD, the plague has begun!" Then Aaron took it as Moses had spoken, and ran into the midst of the assembly, for behold, the plague had begun among the people. So he put on the incense and made atonement for the people. And he took his stand between the dead and the living, so that the plague was checked. But those who died by the plague were 14,700, besides those who died on account of Korah. Then Aaron returned to Moses at the doorway of the tent of meeting, for the plague had been checked.

Numbers 16:46-50

The whole nation of Israel had challenged Moses' leadership; this brought down the anger of the Lord. God told Moses and Aaron to step aside. He did not wait for them to start interceding. He was going to kill this entire people with a plague. Moses and Aaron had no time to think the matter over. Aaron was the priest, the anointed go-between, or mediator, between God and the people; Moses was quickly telling him to literally get into that position between God's outpouring of wrath and the sons of Israel.

In the meantime, the plague was spreading like wildfire. Aaron quickly got his censer (a small golden pot that held burning incense) and went to the very place where the plague was at that moment, and stood there TO STOP THE JUDGMENT BY STANDING BETWEEN THE DEAD AND THE LIVING!

Dangerous? Of course! How are we to know for certain whether God's wrath will stop before it kills us? We can't; we can only trust in the knowledge that as children of God we are already covered by the righteousness of God. That alone may keep the judgment from taking us, and from continuing to take more souls.

Nowhere in this account do we read that God actively looked for the "stand in the gap" man to come between His wrath and the people, as He had done with Sodom and Gomorrah. But He did look! And He gave heed to Aaron's intercession, even though He did not openly call for it. Almost 15,000 people lost their lives from the start of that judgment until the time Aaron took his stand between the dead and the living. Still, many thousands more were saved...not because *they* moved God by entreaty, but because *one man* moved Him by standing in the gap for them. They absolutely did not deserve to live. BUT GOD HATES THE DEATH OF THE WICKED! His eyes are continually searching the prayer closets of cities, looking for those who will do for their cities as Aaron did for his.

Promised Joy, Promised Judgment

Deliver those who are being taken away to death, and those who are staggering to slaughter, Oh hold them back. Proverbs 24:11

As you read this verse, do you see the passion? Do you hear the heartbeat of God? He longs that the wicked choose righteousness so that they might live. He longs for the righteous to lay hold of the lost and dying, to keep them from going to an eternal grave not intended for them. He longs to redeem mankind created in His own image, for we are His children. He is a passionate, loving Father who absolutely hates to see even one soul lost to a forever without Him.

Let him know that he who turns a sinner from the error of his way will save his soul from death, and will cover a multitude of sins.

James 5:20

And have mercy on some, who are doubting; SAVE OTHERS, SNATCHING THEM OUT OF THE FIRE; and on some have mercy with fear, hating even the garment polluted by the flesh.

Jude 22-23

Three

Judgment: The Very First One... With Prophetic Hope

The issue of judgment stirs emotions of a wide range within the hearts of people. It brings up questions in the minds of many: "How could a loving and merciful God allow judgment at all?" "Why does God wait so long to act, while these sinners seem to have a free hand to do whatever they want?" These questions are legitimate, but only for the person who honestly wants an answer.

Too often God Himself is judged by man as unrighteous through such questions because they are asked with angry hearts and closed ears. The Old Testament, in particular, causes many people to stumble over this very issue, viewing the Old Covenant Lord as a big ogre, not as the same God of love and mercy we find in the New Testament. We will look in depth in a later chapter at several judgments poured out which cause very many to stumble over the idea of a merciful God. But we must initially look at the very first time judgment was rendered, with its "unseemly" prophetic hope *for* man.

Promised Joy, Promised Judgment

Only if we rightly understand this first judgment can we begin to understand the character of God; and the reason, based on His character, for the need for judgment; and His heart for man in judgment.

Most people are familiar with the story of Adam and Eve. Adam was the first man created and made in the likeness of God (see Genesis 1:26-28). Adam's name means *man*. Having been made in the image of the Creator meant that the man and his wife were holy, just and clean, all characteristics of their Creator. Adam also had the characteristic of being a good judge of things. This is seen at least partially in the fact that God brought the living creatures to Adam so that he could judge their behavior and thus name them. After his wife was brought to him, Adam also called her what she was: woman. This may seem simplistic, but I believe it shows the confidence that the Creator placed in this creation called "Adam" as he named the rest of the creatures God had created.

Being a good judge connotes being free from bias. We find this scriptural concept set forth clearly throughout the book of Proverbs, among other places. Having the ability to judge rightly also means that one is able to see through deceit in order to correctly discern what is right.

Adam would be tested. Until he ate of the forbidden fruit, Adam was perfect, possessing the godly characteristics of his heavenly Father, including that of good judgment. The challenge given by the adversary was that Adam did *not* have all the wisdom, all the godly characteristics he needed to be able to make sound judgments.

Judgment: The Very First One...With Prophetic Hope

Now the serpent was more crafty than any beast of the field which the LORD God had made. And he said to the woman, "Indeed, has God said…?"
Genesis 3:1

Stop here for a moment and consider the question proposed by the serpent. This question is the root of all unbelief. Indeed, it is the very foundation for skewing true moral judgment. If we can be persuaded that God is not openly honest with us in what He has told us or promised us, according to the truth of what is in the Bible, then we will not walk in sound judgment. If the Judge of all is not honest, then what conviction can a believer in Christ have in trusting even the very work of Jesus on the cross for his justification in the first place?

> *Now the serpent was more crafty than any beast of the field which the LORD God had made. And he said to the woman, "Indeed, has God said, 'You shall not eat from any tree of the garden'?"*
> *And the woman said to the serpent, "From the fruit of the trees of the garden we may eat; but from the fruit of the tree which is in the middle of the garden, God has said, 'You shall not eat from it or touch it, lest you die.'"*
> *And the serpent said to the woman, "You surely shall not die! For God knows that in the day you eat from it your eyes will be opened, and you will be like God, knowing good and evil."*
> *When the woman saw that the tree was good for food, and that it was a delight to the eyes, and that the tree was desirable to make one wise, she*

Promised Joy, Promised Judgment

took from its fruit and ate; and she gave also to her husband with her, and he ate.

Genesis 3:1-6

I have heard it taught that Eve embellished the words of God as she answered the serpent; for nowhere does the Scripture record that God told Adam he and his wife could not even touch the tree. However, I believe she did not embellish His word at all. The woman was as perfect at that point as the day God created her. There was no lie in her; not even the ability to misquote her Creator was in her while she was in that state of perfection. If it were so, then the first sin would not be that they ate the forbidden fruit, but that Adam's wife lied so as to exaggerate the very word of Almighty God, the Creator. I believe the implication that they should not touch the tree was clearly there in Genesis 2:17. How many of us have submitted to temptation by first touching something forbidden before proceeding to bite into that temptation? We shall see that the first judgment against the first sin was not against lying.

When the woman was deceived into thinking that God had not provided all the food she needed, had not given her true vision for her life, and had not given her all the wisdom that she needed, she gave in to the serpent's lying judgment against God. The serpent had convinced her that God knew good and evil in a way that she did not, but that now she could really become like God—if only she would go ahead and eat the forbidden fruit.

But God truly had created Adam, which included his wife, with His exact nature, never *knowing* good and evil (according to the serpent's definition of *"knowing"*).

The *"knowledge of good and evil,"* as spoken of by the serpent, was the *experience* of both good *and* evil. This was knowledge that the serpent alone then possessed. The Creator has never walked in that kind of experiential knowledge. Creator God had certainly not deceived Adam's wife by withholding this knowledge, as the serpent so slyly accused.

When we give in to the temptation to do what God has commanded us not to do, our judgment will be mixed with bias, self-motivation, and those things that corrupt honest or true judgment. And then we will stand condemned every time we render judgment on another.

> *Therefore you are without excuse, every man of you who passes judgment, for in that you judge another, you condemn yourself; for you who judge practice the same things. And we know that the judgment of God rightly falls upon those who practice such things. And do you suppose this, O man, when you pass judgment upon those who practice such things and do the same yourself, that you will escape the judgment of God?*
> Romans 2:1-3

We must understand that judicially there can be no clear flow of relationship between a judge and a convict, except when mercy prevails. There is no question: God is a loving God. But God is also a holy God, wholly pure and clean and without defilement.

Because of this characteristic of God's holiness, we know that Adam and his wife also were created holy. They were made in His image and likeness. But at the very moment they ate the fruit, the defilement that came upon them corrupted the flow of that original perfect relationship. Was it God's condemnation of man that revealed this very barrier between God and man? No! It was a common occurrence of daily fellowship between God and this created couple that revealed this barrier.

> *And they heard the sound of the LORD God walking in the garden in the cool of the day, and the man and his wife hid themselves from the presence of the LORD God among the trees of the garden. Then the LORD God called to the man, and said to him, "Where are you?"*
> *And he said, "I heard the sound of Thee in the garden, and I was afraid because I was naked; so I hid myself."* Genesis 3:8-10

The serpent had told the woman that if she ate of the fruit of the tree of the knowledge of good and evil, she would be like God. But if they had become *like* God, why would they hide *from* God?

The lie of the serpent's statement was now brought to light. Adam had never before hidden himself from God's presence. Was it possible that the two were no longer alike? God had not come into the garden to condemn Adam. He was simply coming to walk with the man and his wife. Yet the simple act of God's showing up to walk with them, as He had often done, made man realize that the flow of fellowship was suddenly not there. In fact, man was doing everything he could do to avoid the very relationship that had previously existed unhindered.

Do you know the saying "Birds of a feather flock together"? In the natural world, people with like interests meet together. They may meet to play golf, or to do business, or to evangelize the nations. But why is this saying true? It is a God thing! This relational flow is from God. Like is drawn unto like, just as Adam and his wife were drawn to God before their sin, for they were like Him!

Thus, the fallacy of the serpent's statement to the woman was that she and her husband would be like God if they ate the forbidden fruit. If that was the case, then why were the created and the Creator not coming together? Because the truth is that they were no longer alike! Death had entered into the relationship. God, the Author of life, and man, originally the recipient of life, were presently no longer alike. This is the definition of death: Death is not first and foremost the nonexistence of life. Rather, death is a severed relationship with the Author of life.

The reciprocal is also true. Eternal life is not simply a living forever. Eternal life is the flow of fellowship through the relationship to the Author of life. Jesus first acknowledged this to be so:

> *"And this is eternal life, that they may know Thee, the only true God, and Jesus Christ whom Thou hast sent."* John 17:3

Life is not walking in an intellectual knowledge of God. Life is experiencing relationship with God—it is *knowing* Him!

Thus we have the predicament in Eden. As the Apostle Paul wrote in Romans 7:24:

> *Wretched man that I am! Who will set me free from the body of this death?*

Promised Joy, Promised Judgment

Because sin had entered into the relationship between God and man, judgment also had to enter in. Judgment was required to remove the obstacles to the relationship between man and His Creator. As paradoxical as it may seem, judgment by God, the Creator, was the very thing needed to set man free.

What is God's nature? He is an almighty and holy God in whose presence sin cannot dwell; but He is also a God of love and mercy toward man. Because of this, God set forth, even in the midst of judgment, a prophetic promise of redemption for man, that mankind might have restored relationship with Him. This would be seen immediately after the Lord rendered judgment in the garden.

Follow the account closely, for herein the character of God regarding judgment is revealed indeed, the very foundation of who He is as the Supreme Judge:

> *Then the L<small>ORD</small> God called to the man, and said to him, "Where are you?"* Genesis 3:9

Was God unaware of what had just taken place between the serpent and this couple? Not at all. He knows all things. But God was pursuing relationship, and He wanted man to know, truly know, that the former relationship was no longer there.

God still seeks after man (see Luke 19:10). He still asks the same question: "Man, where are you?" And it still takes His very presence, His very Spirit, to come to man, in order to make man realize that relationship with His Creator is nonexistent…yet possible…if only man will humble himself and come out of hiding.

Judgment: The Very First One...With Prophetic Hope

> *And He said, "Who told you that you were naked? Have you eaten from the tree of which I commanded you not to eat?"*
>
> *And the man said, "The woman whom Thou gavest to be with me, she gave me from the tree, and I ate."* Genesis 3:11-12

Adam here admits his fault, but points an accusing finger at his wife in the process. Thus his ability to judge rightly is marred.

> *Then the LORD God said to the woman, "What is this you have done?"*
>
> *And the woman said, "The serpent deceived me, and I ate."* Genesis 3:13

Adam's wife—she had not yet been named apart from their oneness as "adam" in their perfection—admits that she was deceived. Genesis 3:6 says she *"saw that the tree was good for food...a delight to the eyes, and... desirable to make one wise."* This may be explained in John's letter in the New Testament: *"...the lust of the flesh and the lust of the eyes and the boastful pride of life"* (1 John 2:16). And so the woman's ability to judge rightly is likewise marred.

> *And the LORD God said to the serpent, "Because you have done this, cursed are you more than all cattle, and more than every beast of the field; on your belly you shall go, and dust shall you eat all the days of your life; and I will put enmity between you and the woman, and between your seed and her seed; he shall bruise you on the head,*

Promised Joy, Promised Judgment

and you shall bruise him on the heel."
                                                    Genesis 3:14-15

We will look further at this judgment on the serpent; however, let us continue in this passage to see the judgment of God as pronounced upon Adam and his wife:

To the woman He said, "I will greatly multiply your pain in childbirth, in pain you shall bring forth children; yet your desire shall be for your husband, and he shall rule over you."

Then to Adam He said, "Because you have listened to the voice of your wife, and have eaten from the tree about which I commanded you, saying, 'You shall not eat from it'; cursed is the ground because of you; in toil you shall eat of it all the days of your life. Both thorns and thistles it shall grow for you; and you shall eat the plants of the field; by the sweat of your face you shall eat bread, till you return to the ground, because from it you were taken; for you are dust, and to dust you shall return."

Now the man called his wife's name Eve, because she was the mother of all the living. And the L<small>ORD</small> *God made garments of skin for Adam and his wife, and clothed them.*
                                                    Genesis 3:16-21

These judgments pronounced by God against Adam and his wife because of their actions were the *just* (judicial) pronouncements of a holy God. He had let them know *while they were in their state of perfection* that they had within their very character the perfect ability to judge and discern for themselves between right and wrong, between life and death. However, it was God's judgment against the serpent that brought a ray of hope to the couple and to their future offspring. This was the first time in history that God showed a side of His character that we all love and need...and need to learn to duplicate: His mercy. If we do not clearly see this aspect of God, we will have a twisted understanding of judgment.

Let us look again at that prophetic hope first promised by God in the judgment pronounced against the serpent:

> *"And I will put enmity between you and the woman, and between your seed and her seed; he shall bruise you on the head, and you shall bruise him on the heel."*   Genesis 3:15

This is a direct reference to a specific future event. The judgment would be felt by the serpent when a seed of the woman, a male Child who would be born in the future, would bruise the serpent on the head. What does this mean? The head speaks of authority. Something would be done by a Male, born to woman, to bring about a blow to the authority of the serpent, who is the devil (see Revelation 12:9). At the fulfillment of this judgment against the serpent, the serpent would strike the heel of this Male.

There are two aspects of this second part of the judgment, *"and you shall bruise him on the heel,"* that we should understand. First, we need to see that this strike is actually the work of the serpent against the seed of the woman. We see this first in the account of two brothers in Genesis. We can see the second aspect when we

Promised Joy, Promised Judgment

look to the Scriptures to see how God views this earth.

This passage brings to mind the story of the birth of Jacob and Esau, as recorded in Genesis chapter 25. It gives us some understanding of the judgment spoken by God against the serpent. As you read the following passage, recall that the male will strike a blow against the authority of the serpent.

> *But the children struggled together within her; and she said, "If it is so, why then am I this way?" So she went to inquire of the L*ORD*.*
>
> *And the L*ORD *said to her, "Two nations are in your womb; and two peoples shall be separated from your body; and one people shall be stronger than the other; and the older shall serve the younger."*
>
> *When her days to be delivered were fulfilled, behold, there were twins in her womb. Now the first came forth red, all over like a hairy garment; and they named him Esau. And afterward his brother came forth WITH HIS HAND HOLDING ON TO ESAU'S HEEL, so his name was called Jacob.*   Genesis 25:22-26a

Jacob's very name means *"one who takes by the heel,"* or, *"one who supplants."* To *supplant* is to take the place of another through deceit, treachery, trickery, scheming and so on. This word comes from a Latin word meaning, "to trip up from beneath," such as taking by the heel in order to pull past another for one's own benefit. Do you see the picture? In the same way, the serpent's intention, when the male seed of the woman would come to bring a blow to his authority, would be to try to supplant the authority of that male.

The second aspect of the judgment, I believe, is intimated by the word *"heel"* in God's pronouncement against the serpent. It is critical that we understand this second aspect, which we will examine more fully later.

The prophet Isaiah proclaimed:

> *Thus says the LORD, "Heaven is My throne, and THE EARTH IS MY FOOTSTOOL...."*
> Isaiah 66:1a

And Jesus Himself said:

> *"But I say to you, make no oath at all, either by heaven, for it is the throne of God, OR BY THE EARTH, FOR IT IS THE FOOTSTOOL OF HIS FEET."* Matthew 5:34-35a

The footstool is where one rests the feet. It is usually the heel that is directly connected to the footstool during that rest. Consequently, the fulfillment of the judgment of God against the serpent would be an event accomplished ON THE EARTH.

In the judgments of Genesis 3, we see the word *cursed* used by God twice. Although Adam and his wife were under the terms of the curse spoken in the judgment by God, God did not use the word *curse* on them. Rather, God told Adam that the ground would be under a curse as a result of his disobedience. This may seem trivial in light of the physical death to follow for all of mankind thereafter. But I believe the fact that the curse was not pronounced directly upon them, as it was pronounced directly onto the serpent, left a glimmer of hope for man. God called the serpent "cursed": *"Cursed are you more than all cattle..."* (Genesis 3:14a). Such wording is not used concerning the devastated couple. There is a certain finality to the pronouncement against the serpent. But that same closed door is not there for the couple. True, their labors would bear a curse because they submitted to, or placed themselves under, the serpent's opinion of God; but the judgment *"Cursed are you..."* was not spoken to them.

God was reaching out as far as infinitely possible to bring about a hope for those created in His image. However, that hope was only extended toward that group, that is, for those created in His image. Let us look further at the prophetic grace that God continued to show forth even after He finished speaking His judgments to the couple.

> *And the LORD God made garments of skin for Adam and his wife, and clothed them.*
> Genesis 3:21

After pronouncing the curse under which they would suffer, God actually covered Adam and his wife, clothing them in the skins of wild animals. Their own efforts to cover themselves did not do away with the feeling of nakedness when God Himself showed up in the garden (see Genesis 3:7-8). This is just like our own efforts whenever we try to cover up our sins. When God shows up, even though He may not come specifically to convict our hearts of the wrong, *His mere presence* is enough to bring us to the realization of the futility of our efforts. We might be able to fool those around us, but we can never deceive our holy God.

True covering for sin can come only from something that God must do for us. This covering that He provided for the young couple in Eden would be a sign of a future event, a shadow of what He would later do for all mankind. Before God could clothe Adam and his wife in the skins, there had to be a sacrifice, a death, a shedding of blood in order to obtain that covering. This was a sign that would be fulfilled millennia later, at Jesus' death, resurrection and ascension. The writer of Hebrews alludes to this:

> *Since therefore, brethren, we have confidence to enter the holy place by the blood of Jesus, by a new and living way which He inaugurated for us through the veil, that is, His flesh...*
> Hebrews 10:19-20

Our confidence to come before God is found as we enter that Holy Place *through Jesus*, whom God provided as a Sacrifice to cover us. We can come by faith into God's presence through the likeness of the veil of the Old Testament Tabernacle.

Finally, there is a prophetic sign by Adam after the judgment. His wife previously had not been given a name because, in their state of perfection, in their unity of covenant together, they were known jointly by one name:

> *And God created man* [lit. "Adam"] *in His own image, in the image of God He created him; male and female He created them.* Genesis 1:27

Just as sin brought about a break in the relationship

between man and his Creator, so it also brought about a break in the unity of the married couple, and even in the unity of their one name. We see this in the man's accusation of his wife in Genesis 3:12. The judgment upon the couple resulted in a sentence of death upon all the descendants of the couple—both physical and spiritual.

However, the hope spoken by God in the judgment of the serpent appears to have planted in the man a seed of faith for that redemption. For it was after the judgment that Adam named his wife Eve, "*because she was the mother of all the living*" (Genesis 3:20). Eve's name means, "*living*" or "*life.*"

The judgment against the serpent rendered an eternal punishment that provided no redemption for the serpent. The serpent had taken away the eternal life, that is, the relationship of man to his Creator.

This first judgment, however, also set in motion a timetable of future prophetic events. A Son would one day be born who would redeem mankind back to that eternal life, that relationship to the One in whose image we were created.

The true character of this Judge in Heaven was established for all time in the eyes of anyone who would reach out, in truth, for needed mercy.

Four

Who Is Judgment Ultimately For?
God's Divine Intention

In a book concerning the judgment of God, it is valid—even necessary—to ask for whom this judgment is ultimately proposed. In other words, what is God's intent in this activity we know as judgment?

First, allow me to clarify: When I ask this question, I am specifically addressing a judgment of condemnation, with absolutely no possibility of redemption. The idea of ultimate condemnation by God is a serious issue; we as the Church must understand who the recipient of such judgment is to be if we are to have an understanding of God's heart for people. If we believe that such judgment is in fact deserved by "those filthy sinners," then it will be easy for us to ask God for judgment to come upon others. However, this attitude also carries consequences that will be personally felt. God does not answer such requests haphazardly. He demands an entirely pure life from those who would pray such prayers, lest judgment overtake the one who prays.

Promised Joy, Promised Judgment

*Seek the L*ORD*, all you humble of the earth who have carried out His ordinances; seek righteousness, seek humility. PERHAPS you will be hidden in the day of the L*ORD*'s anger.*

Zephaniah 2:3

*"Behold, I am going to send My messenger, and he will clear the way before Me. And the Lord, whom you seek, will suddenly come to His temple; and the messenger of the covenant, in whom you delight, behold, He is coming," says the L*ORD *of hosts. "BUT WHO CAN ENDURE THE DAY OF HIS COMING? AND WHO CAN STAND WHEN HE APPEARS? For He is like a refiner's fire and like fullers' soap."* Malachi 3:1-2

The Lord God, in Zephaniah's prophecy above, was *not* guaranteeing safety in the day of the Lord's anger to those who believed they were humble. The implication was clear: Maybe you will be saved, or maybe you won't. Malachi prophesied that the Lord, whom everyone was seeking, was about to show up; but who would be able to stand when He finally appeared?

It is easy to proclaim our own righteousness when we don't look like those around us. But the standard is not the people around us. The standard by which we stand is God Himself!

Glass may look clean after we are through spraying it and wiping it...until a bright light is shone from behind it. Then that glass may show all sorts of streaks and grime. God is like that light. He only judges by the standard of Himself. He is like a refiner's fire and like fullers', or launderers', soap. The refiner's fire and the fullers' soap do not primarily show us what He does, but rather who He is. To understand this and then to receive of His mercy is both to know and to infinitely appreciate a just *and* loving God. The greater the experience of His mercy, the greater the love for the Savior will be (see Luke 7:47). Those who have received of the abundance of His mercy are generally very slow to ask God for judgment upon sinners, no matter how "terrible" the sin.

So then, if God is so desirous to show mercy, for whom is judgment ultimately intended? In fact, why would a merciful and loving God render such judgment? Again, these are legitimate questions that must be asked; yet they must be asked without doubting the integrity of God, without coming to Him with a closed mind that has already determined that there can be no satisfactory answer. God does not answer the mind that does not want an answer in truth, and has already judged Him as unrighteous.

In the previous chapter, we saw that God spoke the word *"curse"* when rendering judgment on the serpent. The root of man's fall came from this one being. Man did have a choice as to whether or not to sin; however, the serpent slyly deceived the woman, and she ate the forbidden fruit and then gave it to her husband who was with her. But the judgment of condemnation by God fell hardest onto the serpent—for God did *not* provide a way of redemption for him.

You see, the ultimate final judgment of condemnation will be on the serpent—the devil, who is Satan—and his angels (see Revelation 20:10). This ultimate judgment will bring to completion the pronouncement of Genesis 3.

Promised Joy, Promised Judgment

The Apostle Peter bears witness to this in the New Testament:

For if God did not spare angels when they sinned, but cast them into hell and committed them to pits of darkness, reserved for judgment...
2 Peter 2:4

The ultimate judgment is an eternal pronouncement against Satan and his angels. Every single one of them is committed *now* to a pit of darkness. They are in prison, if you will, until the final sentence is carried out. There is no parole, no help, no promise of freedom—there is absolutely no hope for them. They are under an eternal sentence of condemnation.

And angels who did not keep their own domain, but abandoned their proper abode, He has kept in eternal bonds under darkness for the judgment of the great day. Jude 6

In the final book of the Bible, John wrote of his vision of the end of this creation and of the new heaven and new earth. Just before he saw this new creation, he witnessed the final judgment. However, John saw an event that took place preceding that judgment.

A great, divinely fierce action is to take place prior to the pronounced final verdicts on souls. Satan, the deceiver, will literally be taken from earth to his eternal damnation. There will be no White Throne judgment for him. His sentence was already and absolutely passed at creation's dawn. Divine intention for judgment which offers no hope whatsoever was cemented back in Eden for the deceiver of men's souls.

> *And the devil who deceived them was thrown into the lake of fire and brimstone...and...will be tormented day and night forever and ever.*
> Revelation 20:10

We know this will be Satan's fate. But we do not yet know the fate of those around us. Satan's goal is to drag them to his end; he will do anything to bring mankind with him. Our goal must be to not give him his desire. To cry out for judgment upon those without Jesus is to ask God to give the devil what he wants. God would have to repent of having required Jesus His Son to pay such a dear price for the salvation of all mankind if He were to grant those kinds of prayers.

I do not mean to imply that no person will go to an eternal judgment of condemnation. Some will, in fact, reject the goodness of God's mercy. But God is their Judge. And this Judge has gone to the greatest lengths to bring salvation to all of mankind. He did this while men were His enemies (see Romans 5:8-10). The eternal judgment that mankind should pay has already been paid for by Christ Jesus His Son (see Romans 6:10). The Jesus who lives within those who have believed in God the Father through what Christ Jesus the Son accomplished is still standing in that place as Mediator for sinners. Jesus said that He came to seek and to save the lost (see Luke 19:10). *He has never ceased from that mission!* He is still seeking, still saving.

The final judgment is ultimately for Satan, the serpent of old. But it will also fall upon those who reject the mercy of the great Judge.

Promised Joy, Promised Judgment

"Then He will also say to those on His left, 'Depart from Me, accursed ones, into the eternal fire WHICH HAS BEEN PREPARED FOR THE DEVIL AND HIS ANGELS...'" Matthew 25:41

Let us be those who walk in God's love, extending that mercy bestowed upon us toward those who "don't deserve it."

FIVE

JUSTICE AND THE LOVE OF GOD: IS THERE A CONFLICT?

"How could a loving God send anyone to Hell?" Have you ever heard this question asked? Have you ever asked it?

I have heard this question several times from different people. Can God be truly just *and* truly loving at the same time and still send people to an eternal damnation?

Years ago I believed that the God of the Old Testament was a cruel God, unlike His character as seen in the New Testament. But how can this be? Did He change? If He did, He would not be consistent! Does the God of the New Testament have a more lax set of rules for those who live after the cross of Jesus? If so, He is not a fair Judge, since He has a double standard of mercy. How can He be fair, yet show grace to those who lived after the cross and condemnation to those who lived prior to it? But if He did *not* change, as some may perceive Him to have done, then why does the New Testament seem to be so lacking in judgments of the type that frequently took place in the Old Testament? Why does it seem that mercy was not so available back then? Was God not a loving God in Old Testament times?

In the book of Exodus, after Israel had left the bondage of slavery in Egypt, God began to speak to Moses the laws that He wanted the people to observe. His basis for giving His people the standard of the Law was His own character. He wanted *His* people to be like *Him*.

Then the LORD spoke to Moses, saying, "Speak to all the congregation of the sons of Israel and say to them, 'You shall be holy, for I the LORD your God am holy.'" Leviticus 19:1-2

The word *"holy"* means "to be clean, free from all defilement." The implication of all the laws given in Exodus and Leviticus is that the nature of the world in which Israel lived was *not* clean, not holy. God did not want the people to continue in the ways they had always known. The character of the people was not like God's character. A character of holiness is the mark of right, or just, standing with God and men. That standard, holiness as God is holy, must originate in the heart first, not in the deeds first, because that standard is in the very heart of God:

Thy throne, O God, is forever and ever; a scepter of uprightness is the scepter of Thy kingdom. THOU HAST LOVED RIGHTEOUSNESS, AND HATED WICKEDNESS; therefore God, Thy God, has anointed Thee with the oil of joy above Thy fellows. Psalm 45:6-7

The writer of the book of Hebrews quoted this passage; however, in Hebrews 1:9 we see the word *"lawlessness"* used in place of *"wickedness."* These two words are used as synonyms (words that have the same definition).

You see, God's very nature is twofold. He does not only love what is right, or only hate what is lawless or wicked. God loves righteousness *and* also hates lawlessness—both at the same time. These are not two separate attributes, but *one* quality. We are the ones who make a distinction between what we perceive to be two separate features. As people, we either hate lawlessness about a matter, or we love righteousness about something else. We do the separating; God does not.

Because of the unified duality of God's nature, with Him is fullness of joy. I believe it is this attribute of God that causes Him to clearly hate sin while yet loving sinners. This oneness of loving righteousness and hating wickedness contains equal passion in that love and hate. God is as passionate about His love for what is right as He is absolutely passionate in His hatred for what is wicked or lawless. (And I believe that if we ever had a clear glimpse of this dual passion in God, we could easily develop a healthy fear of Him.) The goal of God, throughout the entirety of Scripture, is not to get us to "do" holiness, but to "be" holy in our character, as He is holy in His character. The "doing" will follow from this.

God's character is so clean, so holy, that anything that has the slightest defilement would burn up in the fire of His holy presence. God's very character *demands* justice.

> *But the LORD abides forever; He has established His throne for judgment...*   Psalm 9:7

Promised Joy, Promised Judgment

For the L̲o̲r̲d̲ is righteous; He loves righteousness; the upright will behold His face.
Psalm 11:7

He loves righteousness and justice; the earth is full of the lovingkindness of the L̲o̲r̲d̲.
Psalm 33:5

For the L̲o̲r̲d̲ loves justice... Psalm 37:28a

Righteousness and justice are the foundation of Thy throne; lovingkindness and truth go before Thee. Psalm 89:14

When we think about this aspect of God's character and nature, it makes more sense to wonder how such a holy and righteous God could send anyone to Heaven. How could such a just and holy God dwell with any man? But the Scriptures above declare His lovingkindness along with His righteousness. *"Lovingkindness"* is translated as *"mercy"* in the King James Version. This is what makes Him so incredibly wonderful, so absolutely awesome. His character demands justice, yet at the same time pours out mercy. Still, some would ask, "If He has so much mercy to pour out, then how could He send anyone to Hell?"

To answer this, we must look to the Old Testament. Here we find the passages where so many have stumbled over God's judgments, especially those that took place against pagan nations. If we do not see the mercy of God here, we will judge Him as unjust, and so excuse our own lives of sin.

Our basis of study in looking to the Old Testament

judgments is God's character. We will first look at several foundational Scriptures to reveal the true nature of His character in the Old Testament.

> *"Say to them, 'As I live!' declares the Lord GOD, 'I take no pleasure in the death of the wicked, but rather that the wicked turn from his way and live. Turn back, turn back from your evil ways! Why then will you die, O house of Israel?' ...But when the wicked turns from his wickedness and practices justice and righteousness, he will live by them."*
>
> Ezekiel 33:11, 19

> *The Lord is not slow about His promise, as some count slowness, but is patient toward you, not wishing for any to perish but for all to come to repentance.* 2 Peter 3:9

These verses show forth the mercy of God. This is surely not the idea of the God of the Old Testament that many seem to gain from what they've heard concerning those judgments in the Old Covenant Scriptures! However, we will see, based on His character as revealed in the preceding passages, that mercy from God was clearly made available to all who went to their deaths in the midst of judgment. Do you recall the judgment of the cities of Sodom and Gomorrah? Mercy was extended...although the people turned from it.

Let us look more closely at these Old Testament judgments. As we do, continue to keep in your heart Peter's words concerning God's *"slowness"* to judge.

The first major event that was carried out on the

Promised Joy, Promised Judgment

Earth as a judgment against sin was the Flood during the time of Noah. That deluge wiped out all but eight people from our planet. The depravity of mankind had reached the point that man could fall no deeper into the mire of perversion and murder. This perversion is evident from the beginning of Genesis 6:

> *Now it came about, when men began to multiply on the face of the land, and daughters were born to them, that the sons of God saw that the daughters of men were beautiful; and they took wives for themselves, whomever they chose.*
> Genesis 6:1-2

Murder was also quite prevalent on the earth at this time, as we shall see. Such was the decay of society that God, who knows the end from the beginning, at that point in history regretted that He had ever made man:

> *Then the LORD saw that the wickedness of man was great on the earth, and that every intent of the thoughts of his heart was only evil continually. AND THE LORD WAS SORRY THAT HE HAD MADE MAN ON THE EARTH, AND HE WAS GRIEVED IN HIS HEART. And the LORD said, "I will blot out man whom I have created from the face of the land, from man to animals to creeping things and to birds of the sky; for I am sorry that I have made them." ...Now the earth was corrupt in the sight of God, and the earth was filled with violence. And God looked on the earth, and behold, it was corrupt; for all flesh had corrupted their way upon the earth.*
> Genesis 6:5-7, 11-12

Every thought, word and deed of man was *"only evil continually." Only* evil...*continually* evil. The whole earth was *continually violent.* Should we even ask why God would have any sort of mercy whatsoever? But this just God was striving to find justice in man so that He could somehow render mercy. Besides this, He had made a promise to a woman in a garden several generations earlier; that word had yet to be fulfilled.

As we read Genesis chapter 6, we can see that before God says He is sorry that He had created man, before He says that He will blot out the human race, He provides an opportunity for mankind to change.

> *Then the* LORD *said, "My Spirit shall not strive with man forever, because he also is flesh; nevertheless HIS DAYS SHALL BE ONE HUNDRED AND TWENTY YEARS."* Genesis 6:3

God, in His longsuffering, His slowness to judge, His patience, was giving man *"one hundred and twenty years"* to repent. Meditate on that kind of time frame for a moment. "Man, you have one hundred twenty years to change your ways." That is what I call a grace period beyond mercy!

Would mankind have someone to tell them that they needed to change?

> *But Noah found favor in the eyes of the* LORD. *...Noah was a righteous man, blameless in his time; Noah walked with God.*
> Genesis 6:8, 9b

God told Noah His plan—that He was about to destroy every living thing because of the violence of man. The Lord instructed Noah to build an ark, giving him specific directions for the construction of such a vessel. For one hundred twenty years Noah would build that boat. That century-plus construction project, by Noah, proclaimed to the people both the coming judgment and the means of escape.

> *...the patience of God kept waiting in the days of Noah, during the construction of the ark...*
> 1 Peter 3:20

> *...Noah, a preacher of righteousness...*
> 2 Peter 2:5

> *By faith Noah, being warned by God about things not yet seen, in reverence prepared AN ARK for the salvation of his household, BY WHICH HE CONDEMNED THE WORLD...*
> Hebrews 11:7

God was patiently waiting for any who would repent during the one hundred twenty years that Noah was preaching during the period of construction of the ark. Remember the verses we read in Ezekiel 33? God did not desire the death of the wicked in Noah's day. He was not sitting in Heaven anxiously awaiting a time when He could pour out wrath upon man whom He had created in His own image. However, human nature is such that the longer the wait for judgment, the harder the heart becomes if one chooses to wait until a later time to repent. The patient waiting of God does one of two things for man: It gives him an opportunity to change, or it fills the cup of wrath until there is no more room in the cup, at which time God must pour it out as judgment. The choice is not God's. This choice belongs to man!

A week before the Flood, God was still giving opportunity for those around Noah to enter with him into the ark. A supernatural event took place that should have caused the people to seriously take into account what was about to happen.

> *Then the LORD said to Noah, "Enter the ark, you and all your household; for you alone I have seen to be righteous before Me in this time. You shall take with you of every clean animal by sevens, a male and his female; and of the animals that are not clean two, a male and his female; also of the birds of the sky, by sevens, male and female, to keep offspring alive on the face of all the earth. For after seven more days, I will send rain on the earth forty days and forty nights; and I will blot out from the face of the land every living thing that I have made." And Noah did according to all that the LORD had commanded him. ...Then Noah and his sons and his wife and his sons' wives with him entered the ark because of the water of the flood. OF CLEAN ANIMALS AND ANIMALS THAT ARE NOT CLEAN AND BIRDS AND EVERYTHING THAT CREEPS ON THE GROUND, THERE WENT INTO THE ARK TO NOAH BY TWOS, MALE AND FEMALE, AS GOD HAD COMMANDED NOAH.*
>
> Genesis 7:1-5, 7-9

Can you imagine this scene? Every sort of animal, bird, reptile and insect was walking two by two into the

Promised Joy, Promised Judgment

ark! Did it take the full week to get them all in and arranged in their respective places? I don't know. Yet I do know that they all came into the ark to Noah.

Finally, at the end of those seven days, something happened that must have struck fear in the hearts of those who were watching.

> *So they went into the ark to Noah, by twos of all flesh in which was the breath of life. And those that entered, male and female of all flesh, entered as God had commanded him; AND THE LORD CLOSED IT BEHIND HIM.* Genesis 7:15-16

When God closed the door of the ark, mercy's vessel was forever shut to all those outside. Let this sink into your heart, beloved reader—there was absolutely nothing that Noah could do from this point on to help anyone. Family, friends, foes…whomever was outside banging on the door to get in had already made his choice. There was *no more prayer* for mankind. Nothing else could be done.

Was God so unfair, so unjust, so unmerciful when He wiped out an entire planet of life, save the eight people on the ark? No! There had been one hundred twenty years in which the people could have repented and cried out to God to change them…yet they chose not to do so.

When the waters of the Flood finally receded after a year, Noah came out of the ark along with all the living creatures who had entered with him. The planet then contained only eight people. And God Himself came to set forth a law that had not been established among man before this judgment. This law was set up because of what had previously taken place in society. It shows the heart of God in explaining why the Flood had to come, and it warned man not to duplicate that pre-Flood era.

> *"And from every man, from every man's brother I will require the life of man. Whoever sheds man's blood, by man his blood shall be shed, for in the image of God He made man. And as for you, be fruitful and multiply; populate the earth abundantly and multiply in it."* Genesis 9:5b-7

God showed forth His mercy, but the hearts of men spurned it. And so His judgment was poured out.

As man repopulated the earth, his sin, not quite dealt with, spread once more. The next major judgment came against the cities of the valley at the end of the Dead Sea. Among these were Sodom and Gomorrah, of which we have already read. That judgment took place during the life of Abraham.

During that same time, other nations lived within the land promised by God to Abraham. Those nations would be conquered by Joshua several generations later. It is the slaughter of these Canaanite nations by the Hebrews that sometimes causes people to stumble over God. "How could a loving God slaughter innocent women and children?" This becomes the excuse made by some who choose not to follow after God, and it is based on these battles by Joshua and the Hebrews against cities in this land promised to Abraham. Was God planning this slaughter merely so He could give this land to Abraham's descendants? Was there no mercy for these heathen in the heart and mind of God? Let's

Promised Joy, Promised Judgment

find out.

We must begin at a time even farther back than the life of Abraham to see the sin that was established in the land of Canaan. This sin continued to bear fruit through the centuries, mounding up corruption on top of corruption until Joshua's day. To find its beginning, we must return to the post-Flood days of Noah and his family.

According to the Genesis account, Noah and his wife had three sons (see Genesis 6:10). After the Flood, the sons of Noah and their wives had children. Noah's son Ham had four sons, the fourth one named Canaan (see Genesis 10:6). This grandson of Noah, did an act of perversion that set the stage for his direct descendants to follow after in like manner.

> *Then Noah began farming and planted a vineyard. He drank of the wine and became drunk, and uncovered himself inside his tent. And Ham, the father of Canaan, saw the nakedness of his father, and told his two brothers outside. But Shem and Japheth took a garment and laid it upon both their shoulders and walked backward and covered the nakedness of their father; and their faces were turned away, so that they did not see their father's nakedness. When Noah awoke from his wine, he knew what his youngest son had done to him. So he said, "Cursed be Canaan; a servant of servants he shall be to his brothers."*
> Genesis 9:20-25

On the surface of this story, it appears that Ham committed the sin and Canaan took the blame. But I believe the curse reveals that Canaan was involved. Now, Ham was the youngest son of Noah, and Canaan was Ham's youngest son. Sexual perversity in the lineage of Canaan had its roots in this story. Years later, Canaan would father sons who would become nations. If you follow the story in Genesis, you will see clearly what is passed on to the children from generation to generation, until the time of Joshua many hundreds of years later.

And Canaan became the father of Sidon, his firstborn, and Heth and the Jebusite and THE AMORITE and the Girgashite and the Hivite and the Arkite and the Sinite and the Arvadite and the Zemarite and the Hamathite; and afterward the families of the Canaanite were spread abroad. And the territory of the Canaanite extended from Sidon as you go toward Gerar, as far as Gaza; as you go toward Sodom and Gomorrah and Admah and Zeboiim, as far as Lasha.
Genesis 10:15-19

We already know about Sodom and Gomorrah. The people of these cities were descendants of Canaan, Ham's son. Although their sin had filled the cup of wrath by the lifetime of Abraham, it was not so for Canaan's other descendants. In the final ten verses of Genesis 15 we read God's words to Abraham concerning his future descendants. Here we find the Lord's promise that Abraham's descendants would inherit the land of Canaan, which is to say, the land of Canaan's descendants.

Promised Joy, Promised Judgment

> *"And as for you, you shall go to your fathers in peace; you shall be buried at a good old age. Then in the fourth generation they will return here, for THE INIQUITY OF THE AMORITE IS NOT YET COMPLETE."*   Genesis 15:15-16

God promised Abraham that four generations after his death, his descendants would come into the land of Canaan, where Abraham was then sojourning. This was spoken to Abraham before he was eighty-five; and Abraham would live ninety more years (see Genesis 25:7). Isaac and Jacob, son and grandson of Abraham, would live well over a hundred years beyond Abraham's death (see Genesis 35:28; 47:28). Their descendants would live as slaves in Egypt for four hundred thirty more years (see Exodus 12:40). That is a grace period of over *six hundred years* to see change take place in the descendants of Canaan. Would they repent, or would they go from bad to worse? The choice was theirs, not God's. The Lord had even left the ruins of Sodom and Gomorrah intact as a testimony and a warning to the rest of Canaan's descendants of the results of judgment for sin that is not repented.

> *Just as Sodom and Gomorrah and the cities around them, since they in the same way as these indulged in gross immorality and went after strange flesh, ARE EXHIBITED AS AN EXAMPLE, in undergoing the punishment of eternal fire.*
>   Jude 7

Note that Jude wrote in the present tense some 2000 years after that judgment. The ruins of the valley area at the south end of the Dead Sea were obvious to all.

JUSTICE AND THE LOVE OF GOD: IS THERE A CONFLICT?

The area had been lush green, *"like the garden of the LORD,"* the Bible says in Genesis 13:10. Since that horrific morning in Abraham's lifetime, the place stands to this day as an ash heap. Thus the rest of the Canaanites were well warned. *They had no excuse before God for continuing in sin and not knowing its end result!*

Did those Canaanites learn from the ash heap memorial? Did they change their acts? Were they innocent of perversity? Or did they train their children into yet greater sin? What were the Canaanites like six hundred years later when Joshua took the descendants of Abraham in to possess that land? The answer is found in God's instructions to Moses *six hundred years after the fate of Sodom and Gomorrah* concerning the conduct of the Hebrews upon entering Canaan.

> *"You shall not behave thus toward the LORD your God, for every abominable act which the LORD hates they have done for their gods; for they even burn their sons and daughters in the fire to their gods."* Deuteronomy 12:31

> *"When you enter the land which the LORD your God gives you, you shall not learn to imitate the detestable things of those nations. There shall not be found among you anyone who makes his son or his daughter pass through the fire, one who uses divination, one who practices witchcraft, or one who interprets omens, or a sorcerer, or one who casts a spell, or a medium, or a spiritist, or one who calls up the dead."*
> Deuteronomy 18:9-11

> *"You shall not do what is done in the land of*

Egypt where you lived, nor are you to do what is done in the land of Canaan where I am bringing you; you shall not walk in their statutes. ... You shall not uncover the nakedness of a woman and of her daughter, nor shall you take her son's daughter or her daughter's daughter, to uncover her nakedness; they are blood relatives. It is lewdness. ... You shall not lie with a male as one lies with a female; it is an abomination. Also you shall not have intercourse with any animal to be defiled with it, nor shall any woman stand before an animal to mate with it; it is a perversion. Do not defile yourselves by any of these things; for by all these the nations which I am casting out before you have become defiled. For the land has become defiled, therefore I have visited its punishment upon it, so the land has spewed out its inhabitants." Leviticus 18:3, 17, 22-25

This is just a portion of Leviticus 18. The perversion of the inhabitants of the land extended beyond what is quoted above. The land could no longer withstand the filth of moral decay that resulted in even children being offered to the many Canaanite gods. The wickedness of generation after generation had mounted up, since Canaan's perversity toward his grandfather Noah, until there was nothing at all in the fiber of the inhabitants of the land to turn them back.

And yet...even in the midst of all of this, the mercy of God in Heaven, this God of justice, was still made available to anyone who would turn in faith toward Him.

One woman in the first Canaanite city to be taken by

Joshua would save her family from the divine judgment because her heart turned to a God she had never known. The second chapter of Joshua tells the story of two spies sent by Joshua into the city of Jericho before it was conquered by the Israelites. A harlot named Rahab took the two Hebrew spies into her home in order to hide them. Before covering them with some stalks of flax on the roof, she told the two men of the terror of her people toward the Hebrews and their God. When her own people came looking for the spies, knowing they had entered the city, Rahab did not reveal to her people that she had hidden them. Somehow the fear of the Hebrew God caused her heart to turn toward Him, putting her in jeopardy of being caught and killed for treason by her own people. Chapter six of Joshua recounts the overthrow of Jericho. Verse 25 speaks of Rahab's deliverance, along with her family, from her city's destruction...a testimony of the mercy of God in the very midst of judgment.

> *However, Rahab the harlot and her father's household and all she had, Joshua spared; and she has lived in the midst of Israel to this day, for she hid the messengers whom Joshua sent to spy out Jericho.* Joshua 6:25

The awesome mercy and kindness of God is seen in the statement "*...and she has lived in the midst of Israel to this day,*" for Rahab eventually married into the Hebrew line of Judah. And because of this redemption through God's mercy toward her, she is found in the lineage of the Seed of the woman who would bruise the serpent on the head. The New Testament genealogy of

Promised Joy, Promised Judgment

Jesus Christ lists Rahab's name (see Matthew 1:5).

God's mercy extends long periods of grace for man to change. It is not the desire of this holy and just God to send a single soul to an eternity without Him. He is a Father who has created man in His own image. It grieves Him to see the destruction of one made in His image. However, He has also given man a choice: We alone choose whether or not to accept His mercy. His judgments are based on our decisions.

This same principle is true of my children. They choose to do wrong or right. If they choose the former, they know the consequence, which is discipline. And if they continue on in that place of rebellion, the discipline also becomes greater, more severe. It is not because I hate them that I discipline them; it is because I love them. If I do not correct them, they will grow up to become tomorrow's prison inmates.

The excuse by people not to turn to God because He has allowed the slaughter of "the innocent" is usually made by those who want to continue in *their own* sin. Because of this, they reach for any excuse, however feeble, to keep God from pointing His finger at their sin. If God was the kind of father who did not care about His people, He would not bother to correct them. Yet societies left to their own ways corrupt equally in both moral decay and violence, as the testimonies of the two societies spoken of in this chapter bear witness.

The God of the Old Testament is the same God of the New Testament. His character still demands justice and still pours out mercy. It is each individual's choice whether to stand in His judgment...or stand in His mercy.

Six

Longing for the Justice of God...and the Souls of Men

*Therefore the L*ORD *longs to be gracious to you, and therefore He waits on high to have compassion on you. For the L*ORD *is a God of justice; how blessed are all those who long for Him.*

Isaiah 30:18

It is easy to understand and to personally desire the mercy of a holy and just God. It can also be easy to understand when circumstances cause one to cry out for the justice of God against those who walk in wickedness continually, even when the wicked are shown kindness and goodness.

But can one have a heart to cry for justice and simultaneously desire the salvation of the souls of the unjust, without having a heart of duplicity? Can one desire mercy without being so overly "merciful" that it cancels out the justice necessary to turn such hearts to God? Indeed, the times in which we live demand that a just God act, lest all mankind wonder if there is a God at all because of the rapid increase in lawlessness. Yet this same age also cries out for God to win the souls of mankind to right and just ways, lest the work of God through His Son's cross appear to be a failure.

Might we not just as well despair of mankind, crying out to God to take away those who are already believers, leaving the rest of the earth to rot? Some would say yes. But we must remember that God says that every single person was His enemy—which includes present-day believers—and that He poured out His love to all anyway through the death of His Son (see Romans 5:8-10). Yet even so, He poured out His mercy and love upon mankind. And so the question remains: Can we long for God's needed justice *and* still yearn for the salvation of men's souls? Can God pour out judgment in a way that brings men and women to their knees in repentance without destroying them?

Isaiah's words, quoted above, tell us that this God of justice is waiting to show compassion. Isaiah even went so far as to say that those who desire this God of justice are blessed. We must see these two concepts as related together: "God of justice, pour out Your justice *and* compassion." But how can He do this?

The slowness of God to judge, as we have already seen, is the patience of God waiting for men to come to a place of repentance. Yet that same slowness of God to judge can have an opposite result when hearts refuse to bend the knee.

> *Or do you think lightly of the riches of His kindness and forbearance and patience, not knowing that the kindness of God leads you to repentance?*
> Romans 2:4

The answer to this question sometimes is yes. There is something in stubborn man that refuses to regard the kindness and the patience of God. Instead of turning from wickedness, the lack of God's judgment is taken advantage of in order to perpetrate more selfishness, greed, lust, sin. Thus God has to revert to seasons of judgment to awaken sinful man. (Note that I did not write "condemnation", but "judgment.") I believe God wants His people to long for His justice in order to turn men's hearts toward Him.

> *O Upright One, make the path of the righteous level. Indeed, while following the way of Thy judgments, O LORD, we have waited for Thee eagerly; Thy name, even Thy memory, is the desire of our souls. At night my soul longs for Thee, indeed, my spirit within me seeks Thee diligently; for when the earth experiences Thy judgments the inhabitants of the world learn righteousness. Though the wicked is shown favor, he does not learn righteousness; he deals unjustly in the land of uprightness, and does not perceive the majesty of the LORD.* Isaiah 26:7b-10

Isaiah's prayers were times of looking to the Lord for His judgments. Why? Because he had seen that God's favor had *not* caused the wicked to turn to Him. Instead, they acted even more unjustly. Isaiah knew that sinners sometimes repent only if they experience the judgments of God. Look again at the name he called God: "*Upright One.*" Isaiah's desire in his prayer was to see the Upright One. This name possesses the character that God desires to be in man. And this character is what

Promised Joy, Promised Judgment

Isaiah eagerly prayed for when he asked that God be revealed in righteous judgments. Isaiah had already made sure that his own steps had been according to God's judgments of the past; that is, Isaiah had sought to walk in uprightness himself based on how God had previously judged. Yet the people of his day had forgotten those past judgments, even as the Canaanites had forgotten to take seriously the ash heaps of several of their own cities.

Isaiah did not ask for utter destruction of a city or people. But he did ask for judgments that would cause peoples' hearts to cry out to God for mercy and thus be changed. Even as he prayed for judgment, Isaiah was telling the people that God longed to pour out compassion on them. However, sometimes one must *experience* righteous judgment before he can bring himself to long for the Judge's compassion.

> *Ephraim is oppressed, crushed in judgment, because he was determined to follow man's command. Therefore I am like a moth to Ephraim, and like rottenness to the house of Judah. When Ephraim saw his sickness, and Judah his wound, then Ephraim went to Assyria and sent to King Jareb. But he is unable to heal you, or to cure you of your wound. For I will be like a lion to Ephraim, and like a young lion to the house of Judah. I, even I, will tear to pieces and go away, I will carry away, and there will be none to deliver. I will go away and return to My place until they acknowledge their guilt and seek My face; in their affliction they will earnestly seek Me.*
>
> Hosea 5:11-15

What may seem difficult to comprehend is that God's judgment does not drive man away from Him, but toward Him. In the world we shun those who discipline us severely. But the God of justice is a God who also embodies lovingkindness. God allowed severe judgment to come to the Israeli tribes of Judah and Ephraim; yet their prayer afterward was that of a repentant heart:

> *"Come, let us return to the LORD. For He has torn us, but He will heal us; He has wounded us, but He will bandage us. He will revive us...."*
>
> Hosea 6:1-2a

Another judgment which brought severe discipline to Judah is recorded in the book of Joel. Because the sons of Israel chose to walk after their own ways, God sent army after army of locusts to utterly devastate the land...so that the inhabitants could once again learn righteousness. However, God did not afterward leave the people on their own to sort out how to heal their environment. He came to them with a word of encouragement that if they would humble themselves, He would heal their land so much so that...

> *...the threshing floors will be full of grain, and the vats will overflow with the new wine and oil. ..."And you shall have plenty to eat and be satisfied, and praise the name of the LORD your God."*
>
> Joel 2:24, 26

The judgment that came upon the people drove them back to God, not away from Him.

We can long for the justice of God in our prayers, with

the understanding that His love of justice does not work against His love for man. God's love of justice fuels His desire to see man transformed more and more into the image of Christ and walking in His lovingkindness and righteousness.

Look at the words of Jesus concerning believers' prayers for their "enemies":

> *"You have heard that it was said, 'Y<small>OU SHALL LOVE YOUR</small> <small>NEIGHBOR</small>, and hate your enemy.' But I say to you, love your enemies, and pray for those who persecute you in order that you may be sons of your Father who is in heaven."* Matthew 5:43-45a

The command of the Lord is to pray *for* our enemies, not against them...*so that we can be like our Father in Heaven.* The Apostle Paul explained that these prayers *for* people can even bring about justice and righteousness within society:

> *First of all, then, I urge that entreaties and prayers, petitions and thanksgivings, be made on behalf of all men, for kings and all who are in authority, IN ORDER THAT WE MAY LEAD A TRANQUIL AND QUIET LIFE IN ALL GODLINESS AND DIGNITY. This is good and acceptable in the sight of God our Savior, who desires all men to be saved and to come to the knowledge of the truth. For there is one God, and one mediator also between God and men, the man Christ Jesus, who gave Himself as a ransom for all....*
> 1 Timothy 2:1-6a

This word *"mediator"* that Paul used is a judicial term. It describes a go-between who acts between two opposing parties to bring about a settlement in a dispute. God is the Judge and Opposer of all who walk in sin. This passage from Paul's letter to Timothy instructs us to pray *for* men, not against them. Why? Because the Mediator has opened the way for reconciliation between the two opposing parties! Christ our Mediator has mediated the dispute between man and God by giving Himself as the settlement for the verdict against man.

I believe we need to cry out for justice more than we do, in order to see the Lord's right and just ways increase in the earth. However, our prayers absolutely must be tempered with God's mercy for mankind.

SEVEN

DESIRING JUDGMENT ON A CITY VERSUS THE HEART OF GOD

Everyone seems to know that judgment is coming. But I think that as much as we are looking to Heaven for God to "start judgin'," He is looking to our heart attitudes toward the wicked, the lost, those who hold no claim to Christ whatsoever.

When watching the nightly news or reading the newspapers, certain cities seem to be continually cited as the worst places to live. Statistics show them to have the most numerous or most violent crimes. When I was growing up, I remember hearing of Detroit as having a very high number of murders. Cities such as Los Angeles and Miami have stood out as cities of riots. New York has been known as a city of gangs. Each of us could name cities that have such labels in our minds…and it seems only right to cry out for judgment, because judgment has a purging attribute.

Promised Joy, Promised Judgment

There were times when men of God in the Bible called for judgment on cities. They apparently felt that these cities should suffer the same fate as Sodom and Gomorrah.

> *And it came about, when the days were approaching for His ascension, that He resolutely set His face to go to Jerusalem; and He sent messengers on ahead of Him. And they went, and entered a village of the Samaritans, to make arrangements for Him. And they did not receive Him, because He was journeying with His face toward Jerusalem. And when His disciples James and John saw this, they said, "Lord, do You want us to command fire to come down from heaven and consume them?"* Luke 9:51-54

Here we see the very Son of God, a Man doing awesome miracles, being rejected by a small city. The only reason given for this rejection is that He was traveling on to Jerusalem; for the Samaritans of that little city did not care for the people of Jerusalem. The Samaritans and the Jews, especially of Jerusalem, were constantly at odds with one another. The Samaritans were not about to allow anyone to spend the night in their city who intended to go to Jerusalem on business the following day. The rivalry was hot. These people did not care whether this Man was the Son of God or not. (The Samaritans also did not know that Jerusalem was about to reject this same Man; if they had, they might have taken Him in just to spite the people of Jerusalem.)

But two of Jesus' disciples, who had seen and participated in the mighty miracles He had done, were annoyed with this Samaritan village. (I think they might have carried a bit of the antagonism of the Jews against the Samaritans). "After all," they probably reasoned, "How dare these Samaritans reject the Messiah (who just happened to be pure Jewish)? Who do they think they are? We'll show them!"

Please hear this with your heart, beloved. These disciples were more interested in what was "right" than with mercy, even if it meant sending men to a fiery Hell. They wanted judgment, immediate judgment; there was absolutely no thought of mercy in their hearts. You see, when one has not experienced the depths of God's mercy, one can easily cry out for judgment. It is those who have known the depths of God's forgiveness who are extremely slow to ask for judgment. But look at the heart of God for this tiny city that rejected His mercy:

> *But He turned and rebuked them, [and said, "YOU DO NOT KNOW WHAT KIND OF SPIRIT YOU ARE OF; for the Son of Man did not come to destroy men's lives, but to save them."]*
> Luke 9:55-56a

So compassionate was the heart of God for this village of people who refused to receive His only Son that Jesus rebuked two of His own disciples for even considering the destruction of this small town. God saw that hope still existed for these people. And He wanted to demonstrate to *His people* His heart, His reason for sending His Son. God is not a God who changes. Do you believe in Jesus? I say to you that the Son of Man is still coming to towns, villages, cities and megalopolises, seeking to save men's lives.

Promised Joy, Promised Judgment

What spirit are you of? Does your heart move in the direction of Jesus' heart for cities full of crime and perversion and all sorts of evil, cities that have not yet seen God's power at work in them? *What spirit are you of?* The Holy Spirit in Jesus wanted salvation for this small city of Samaritans. Is your spirit in agreement with the Holy Spirit for those who walk in the unholiness of sin?

There was another man of God, a prophet who had the word of God strongly in his mouth; but he was a man of like spirit to John and James. This man lived centuries prior to Jesus' disciples. The city against which he had set his heart was also a foreign city, but it was much, much greater in size and population than the Samaritan village.

> *The word of the* Lord *came to Jonah the son of Amittai saying, "Arise, go to Nineveh the great city, and cry against it, for their wickedness has come up before Me."* Jonah 1:1-2

And what was the message that Jonah was to cry against this great city?

> *"Yet forty days and Nineveh will be overthrown."* Jonah 3:4b

Those eight words were the only words Jonah was to speak to the city—no apparent room for mercy here, no room for forgiveness, and none for repentance. *"Forty days and Nineveh will be overthrown."* This was very cut and dried and dreadfully to the point.

And, boy, was that man of God ever pleased!

Everyone knows the story of Jonah and the whale; or

Desiring Judgment on a City Versus the Heart of God

at least we think we know it. Why was this man of God swallowed by the fish? Was he running from God...or from the heart of God?

> *But Jonah rose up to flee to Tarshish from the presence of the L*ORD*. So he went down to Joppa, found a ship which was going to Tarshish, paid the fare, and went down into it to go with them to Tarshish from the presence of the L*ORD*. And the L*ORD *hurled a great wind on the sea and there was a great storm on the sea so that the ship was about to break up. Then the sailors became afraid, and every man cried to his god, and they threw the cargo which was in the ship into the sea to lighten it for them. But Jonah had gone below into the hold of the ship, lain down, and fallen sound asleep. So the captain approached him and said, "How is it that you are sleeping? Get up, call on your god. Perhaps your god will be concerned about us so that we will not perish."*
> Jonah 1:3-6

This passage clearly reveals both the character of Jonah and the character of the lost. Jonah could not have cared less about "those pagans" running the ship, whether they died or not. But it was "those pagans" who understood something of the possibility of Jonah's God. They understood, when Jonah apparently did not, that his God might be a divinity who possessed some sort of mercy. They understood, even if Jonah did not care, that if the man of God were to call upon Him, He might save the whole lot of them.

Do you hear what I am saying, beloved? The lost

know there is a God of mercy, and they are asking for those who know this God to ask Him for them. Are you asleep on the boat? Do you care about those who will drown in sin? Did you forget that mercy was once shown to you?

Jonah was running from God simply to run from God. He feared God. He said as much in verse 9. How was it that this prophet could run from God, allow this calamity to come upon them, and then not even care that they were all about to perish for his running away? They finally asked Jonah what they should do to stop the storm that raged all around them. He told them that if they would throw him into the sea, the storm would stop.

But these men showed mercy on him who couldn't have cared less about them!

> *And he said to them, "Pick me up and throw me into the sea. Then the sea will become calm for you, for I know that on account of me this great storm has come upon you." However, the men rowed desperately to return to land but they could not, for the sea was becoming even stormier against them.*
>
> *THEN THEY CALLED ON THE LORD and said, "We earnestly pray, O LORD, do not let us perish on account of this man's life and do not put innocent blood on us; for Thou, O LORD, hast done as Thou hast pleased."* Jonah 1:12-14

These pagans were willing to place their own lives in jeopardy in a desperate attempt to save the life of this man of God. Then *they* called on the Lord his God for themselves. Nowhere throughout the saga of the storm do we read of Jonah crying out to God on their behalf. *The pagans did Jonah's job!*

It would be three days before Jonah finally lifted up his voice to the Almighty. Yet even then, he did not seek to receive God's heart for Nineveh. And what had he just witnessed? The Lord showed mercy to the pagans on the ship, and *they believed in Him and feared Him for it!* (See Jonah 1:16.)

God got Jonah's attention—not his heart, just his attention.

God spared Jonah from perishing in the belly of the whale after he had been thrown out of the ship and then swallowed by the great fish. But I don't believe that fish was sent just to save Jonah. When I read this passage, I see God gazing down upon a huge metropolis that was soon to suffer the same fate as Sodom.

After God freed him from the fish, Jonah grudgingly obeyed God and headed off to Nineveh. Then Jonah reluctantly, with half a heart, carried out the proclamation of God's word to the city. Do you recall his message? It was not a proclamation for repentance, but of coming judgment.

> *Now Nineveh was an exceedingly great city, a THREE DAYS' WALK. Then Jonah began to go through the city ONE DAY'S WALK; and he cried out and said, "Yet forty days and Nineveh will be overthrown."*   Jonah 3:3b-4

Jonah could honestly say that he went to the city and cried out precisely what God had told him. But his half-heartedness is clearly seen in that he did not walk for three days throughout the length of the city to let all the people know what was about to happen.

However, Jonah's one-day effort was enough

"leaven," if you will, for God to spread the message throughout the city—all the way to the king.

> *Then the people of Nineveh believed in God; and they called a fast and put on sackcloth from the greatest to the least of them. When the word reached the king of Nineveh, he arose from his throne, laid aside his robe from him, covered himself with sackcloth, and sat on the ashes. And he issued a proclamation and it said, "In Nineveh by the decree of the king and his nobles: Do not let man, beast, herd, or flock taste a thing. Do not let them eat or drink water. But both man and beast must be covered with sackcloth; and let men call on God earnestly that each may turn from his wicked way and from the violence which is in his hands. Who knows, God may turn and relent, and withdraw His burning anger so that we shall not perish?" When God saw their deeds, that they turned from their wicked way, then God relented concerning the calamity which He had declared He would bring upon them. And He did not do it.* Jonah 3:5-10

The people of the great city believed the preaching of this man who had cared so little for their lives. And again, these pagans cried out in complete humility to a God who was not their god. Although the prophetic proclamation made absolutely no mention of possible repentance, the wicked citizens of this massive city responded to the impending judgment anyway, believing that maybe the God of this preacher would change His mind. And the great and merciful God of justice saw

Desiring Judgment on a City Versus the Heart of God

and listened to their humble repentance. The heart of God is seen as He relents from the promised destruction.

It is here that we also see the initial reason that the man of God ran in the opposite direction when he had been given the commission to come to Nineveh. His reaction shows of what kind of spirit Jonah was.

> *But it greatly displeased Jonah, and he became angry. And he prayed to the Lord and said, "Please Lord, was not this what I said while I was still in my own country? Therefore, in order to forestall this I fled to Tarshish, for I knew that Thou art a gracious and compassionate God, slow to anger and abundant in lovingkindness, and one who relents concerning calamity. Therefore now, O Lord, please take my life from me, for death is better to me than life."* Jonah 4:1-3

Now we see why Jonah chose to disobey the very God he said he feared. And we see why he slept while the pagans on the ship cried out to their god first, and then to Jonah's God to have mercy on them and stop the storm. Jonah was very willing to die on that ship. If the captain had not come down and wakened him from his slumber, Jonah would have slept all the way to the bottom of the sea. Jonah knew that when he proclaimed destruction to the great city, they might repent. He knew enough of God to understand that if that happened, God would have mercy.

And Jonah did not want that to happen.

Jonah hated Nineveh. He very much wanted judgment. He wanted these despicable sinners to perish. But Ninevah was spared!

Promised Joy, Promised Judgment

Then God turned His attention to demonstrating His heart to His prophet.

*And the L*ORD *said, "Do you have good reason to be angry?"* Jonah 4:4

Then Jonah went out from the city and sat down to the east of it, at a place with a good view of Nineveh. There he made a shelter for himself and sat under it in shaded comfort so that he could watch what would happen in the city.

Although the prophet knew that God had relented from sending the judgment, in his heart of hearts Jonah still hoped that his word of judgment would come to pass, that the city would be destroyed. So he spent the remainder of the forty days he had prophesied east of the city on a hill in order to watch the spectacle at the end of those days.

*So the L*ORD *God appointed a plant and it grew up over Jonah to be a shade over his head to deliver him from his discomfort. And Jonah was extremely happy about the plant. But God appointed a worm when dawn came the next day, and it attacked the plant, and it withered. And it came about when the sun came up that God appointed a scorching east wind, and the sun beat down on Jonah's head so that he became faint and begged with all his soul to die, saying, "Death is better to me than life."*

Then God said to Jonah, "Do you have a good reason to be angry about the plant?"

And he said, "I have good reason to be angry, even to death."

DESIRING JUDGMENT ON A CITY VERSUS THE HEART OF GOD

Then the LORD said, "You had compassion on the plant for which you did not work, and which you did not cause to grow, which came up overnight and perished overnight. AND SHOULD I NOT HAVE COMPASSION ON NINEVEH, the great city in which there are more than 120,000 persons who do not know the difference between their right and left hand, as well as many animals?"

Jonah 4:6-11

The book of Jonah ends with this word from God to His prophet. Does more need to be said about the heart of God?

Eight

A Cry for Unrighteous Leaders

Paul the apostle made a most profound statement to Timothy during the days of the wicked rulers of the Roman Caesars.

> *First of all, then, I urge that entreaties and prayers, petitions and thanksgivings, be made on behalf of all men, for kings and all who are in authority, in order that we may lead a tranquil and quiet life in all godliness and dignity. This is good and acceptable in the sight of God our Savior, who desires all men to be saved and to come to the knowledge of the truth.*
> 1 Timothy 2:1-4

Paul's command was that we should pray earnestly *for* our governmental leaders. When we consider the period in which he lived, his statement is quite astounding.

Yet for those of us living today in nations with far more moderate governments, this command ought to

Promised Joy, Promised Judgment

be taken much more seriously than it often is. Nations are ruled by men. Cities are ruled by men. And God's heart is for all men, which includes all government leaders, to believe in Jesus Christ. The benefit of having godly leaders, for both nations and cities, is a life of tranquility and quietness. In other words, prayers for the peace of God to rule through the leaders who rule will bring back returns of peace upon the one who prays (see Jeremiah 29:7). Such prayer also opens the city or nation for God's Kingdom to be established in men's hearts.

There is therefore a call to pray *for* political leaders, national and local, and for the salvation of all in nations and cities. But there is no corresponding call to abandon the great metropolises to Hell. Many people today want to move to the suburbs outside the cities because of the increase in lawlessness within the cities. Crime follows, however, in time...and families move still farther out, until again the city and all its evils catch up with them.

We have seen what a move of God could do in a short time to change the atmosphere of even the most wicked of cities. Nineveh changed because leaders from that city understood what judgment upon their city would mean without repentance. To abandon a city in hopes of gaining God's judgment against it is to look like Jonah. To cry out to God *for* your city, *for* its leadership, *for* its welfare, is to look like God.

King Solomon, the governmental leader of Israel in the Old Testament, spoke of those who bless their cities and those who curse them:

By the blessing of the upright a city is exalted, but

A Cry for Unrighteous Leaders

by the mouth of the wicked it is torn down.
                                   Proverbs 11:11

If this alone is the standard of uprightness or wickedness, how does each of us measure up? Do we bless our cities, or do we tear them down with that which comes out of our mouths? We set the standard of city leadership in part through voting. That's valuable.

Paul never had that luxury. But he did have something that never went out of date. He prayed. He earnestly prayed with…*"entreaties and prayers, petitions and thanksgivings,"* because he knew that these kinds of prayers would have a twofold benefit: a tranquil life for the citizens, and eternal life through the salvation of those leaders. We cannot wait for elections to change unrighteous leaders. We are commanded to pray *for* them, not *against* them.

The Old Testament presents the exemplary life of a man who earnestly desired salvation and godly leadership for the king he diligently served, a king steeped in pagan worship. This godly man made sure that the leader he served knew that he himself feared the God of Heaven, that all wisdom and understanding for leadership came from his God, and that this leader's right to rule also came from that same God. To do this man justice, one would have to read his life story in its entirety from the Old Testament book that bears his name. However, here we shall only look at some aspects of the life of Daniel.

Throughout most of Daniel's life, the greatest known empire on earth was the nation of Babylon, under the rule of King Nebuchadnezzar. Among the nations King Nebuchadnezzar had conquered and relocated (into slavery) was the nation of Israel. Daniel was taken along with the exiles from Jerusalem to Babylon, probably as a teenager (see Daniel 1), and he was trained in the language and culture of the Babylonians and brought into direct service to King Nebuchadnezzar. In the second year of King Nebuchadnezzar's reign, the king had a dream that he could not let go of after he awoke. He was puzzled by it and wanted to understand its meaning.

What was strange about the king's dream is this: He knew that the dream was significant, but he couldn't remember exactly what it was that he had dreamed. So he called in all the wise men and magicians of his empire. They were not only to interpret the dream, but to first tell the king what exactly it was that he had dreamed. No one among all of his political advisors, however deeply into magic they might have been, was able to fulfill this demand. They asked the king to tell them what he had dreamed, promising that they would then interpret it for him. This angered the king. He ordered all of these "wise men" to be killed. Although Daniel had not been summoned, he was nonetheless one of the king's advisors, and so was part of the roster for execution.

When Daniel heard of the king's decree, he requested a few days to seek his God for the answer. When this was approved, he gathered three friends together to pray with him for the answer—but not for his own sake, that he would not be killed; *he asked on behalf of the king.* God made known to Daniel the dream and its interpretation. Daniel immediately took this divine word to King Nebuchadnezzar.

The king answered and said to Daniel, whose

name was Belteshazzar, "Are you able to make known to me the dream which I have seen and its interpretation?" Daniel 2:26

What an opportunity for Daniel to get a swelled head! What a great time to exalt himself! He was the only person who could relate the dream to the king—but only because God had let him know what the dream was. But Daniel was not looking for self-exaltation. His desire was that this pagan leader come to believe in his God. He did not venture to try to force his faith onto the king, but patiently gave his testimony with much godly wisdom and prudence. Let's look at a few portions of Daniel's response that show his heart for this wicked king.

Daniel answered before the king and said, "As for the mystery about which the king has inquired, neither wise men, conjurers, magicians, nor diviners are able to declare it to the king. However, THERE IS A GOD IN HEAVEN WHO REVEALS MYSTERIES, AND HE HAS MADE KNOWN TO KING NEBUCHADNEZZAR what will take place in the latter days. This was your dream and the visions in your mind while on your bed.... You, O king, are the king of kings, TO WHOM THE GOD OF HEAVEN HAS GIVEN THE KINGDOM, the power, the strength, and the glory; and wherever the sons of men dwell, or the beasts of the field, or the birds of the sky, HE HAS GIVEN THEM INTO YOUR HAND AND HAS CAUSED YOU TO RULE OVER THEM ALL. ..."
Daniel 2:27-28, 37-38

Promised Joy, Promised Judgment

Daniel had prayed to his God for his king, and God graciously gave him the answers the king sought. When Daniel went before the king, he first acknowledged his God before him, and explained to the ruler that the answer to his request could *only* have come from the God of Heaven. Finally, Daniel spoke forth the dream and its interpretation.

And the outcome…

> *The king answered Daniel and said, "SURELY YOUR GOD IS A GOD OF GODS and a Lord of kings and a revealer of mysteries, since you have been able to reveal this mystery."*
>
> Daniel 2:47

Daniel could have been arrogant before the king, full of religious pride. But Daniel understood that leadership was not his to take. Yet even beyond this, I believe Daniel recognized the *full authorization by God of this pagan leader's power*, and he also realized that this man *did not know* that truth.

Some time later, the king dreamed another dream, which disturbed him much more than the first had. As Daniel stood in the throne room listening to the king recount his dream—this king who had yet to submit his heart to the God of Heaven—God was making known the interpretation to Daniel. Again, the pure heart of Daniel *for* this leader is revealed.

> *"Then Daniel, whose name is Belteshazzar, was appalled for a while as his thoughts alarmed him. The king responded and said, 'Belteshazzar, do not let the dream or its interpretation alarm you.'*

A Cry for Unrighteous Leaders

"Belteshazzar answered and said, 'MY LORD, IF ONLY THE DREAM APPLIED TO THOSE WHO HATE YOU, AND ITS INTERPRETATION TO YOUR ADVERSARIES!'" Daniel 4:19

Daniel realized, as God was showing him the interpretation of the king's dream, that something dreadful had been determined by God as a judgment against this pagan leader; and because of this, Daniel was *"appalled"* and *"alarmed."*

How many of us, knowing something terrible was to happen to our national or local unbelieving political leader, would honestly have the same heart as Daniel had for Nebuchadnezzar? Or would we rejoice? This is not to bring condemnation, beloved, if your heart does not feel compassion toward your leaders; but this is a call to ask God to change your heart. Seek the Lord, that He might make your heart into the image of Christ and that He might give you His mind for your leaders in government. Remember the scripture quoted at the beginning of this chapter:

> *First of all, then, I urge that entreaties and prayers, petitions and thanksgivings, be made on behalf of...all who are in authority.... This is good and acceptable in the sight of God our Savior, who desires all men to be saved and to come to the knowledge of the truth.*
> 1 Timothy 2:1-4

Let us read Daniel's final counsel to the king as he told him of what was about to happen to him:

Promised Joy, Promised Judgment

> *" 'Therefore, O king, may my advice be pleasing to you: break away now from your sins by doing righteousness, and from your iniquities by showing mercy to the poor, in case there may be a prolonging of your prosperity.' "* Daniel 4:27

Daniel desired the salvation and prosperity of this pagan leader.

Nebuchadnezzar would eventually forget Daniel's final counsel. And so the matter came about from God to greatly humble the king by causing him to live as an animal for a long season of time. But when that season came to an end, this pagan king again acknowledged Daniel's God.

> *"Now I Nebuchadnezzar praise, exalt, and honor the King of heaven, for all His works are true and His ways just, and He is able to humble those who walk in pride."* Daniel 4:37

This is the goal of crying out to God *for* unrighteous leaders!

> *The king's heart is like channels of water in the hand of the LORD; He turns it wherever He wishes.*
> Proverbs 21:1

I believe that if the people of God, who say that God can do anything, would pray together as one man *for* their leaders, even as Paul said that we ought to do, we would see God use those prayers in a great way to change the course of our society. We would see God turn the hearts of unrighteous leaders to accomplish His

A Cry for Unrighteous Leaders

purposes for the areas they rule. We would see more situations like that of Nineveh in Jonah's day. We would see leaders like King Nebuchadnezzar make proclamations similar to his.

I think one of the most spectacular transformations of an extremely wicked governmental leader is the Old Testament story of King Manasseh. I personally believe him to be one of *the* most wicked leaders in biblical history. He was a man who knew what was right and acceptable to God, yet he absolutely, wholeheartedly, unabashedly set his heart to fulfill all the conceivable wickedness known to the pagan world, and he was maybe even worse than many of the pagan kings before him…but God hates the death of the wicked.

> *Manasseh was twelve years old when he became king, and he reigned fifty-five years in Jerusalem. And he did evil in the sight of the LORD according to the abominations of the nations whom the LORD dispossessed before the sons of Israel.*
> 2 Chronicles 33:1-2

What did this king do that was so very bad? He rebuilt the high places that had been broken down; he erected altars for the false gods of the region, including the Baals, and he set up Asherim; he worshiped *"all the host of heaven."* He even built altars—and later set up an idol—in the House of the Lord itself at which to worship other gods! Not only this, but he sacrificed his own sons and practiced witchcraft and other forms of occultic activity.

> *Thus Manasseh misled Judah and the inhabitants*

> *of Jerusalem to do more evil than the nations whom the LORD destroyed before the sons of Israel. And the LORD spoke to Manasseh and his people, but they paid no attention.*
>
> 2 Chronicles 33:9-10

So evil was this leader that God purposed to judge the nation, cleaning it just as one would a dish, and wiping away all the filth, thus abandoning His promise to keep the people in the land. But even this was not enough to halt the wicked deeds of Manasseh. After reading the following passage, you will wonder whether there was even a remote possibility that God could have any mercy for this man.

> *Now the LORD spoke through His servants the prophets, saying, "Because Manasseh king of Judah has done these abominations, having done wickedly more than all the Amorites did who were before him, and has also made Judah sin with his idols; therefore thus says the LORD, the God of Israel, 'Behold, I am bringing such calamity on Jerusalem and Judah, that whoever hears of it, both his ears shall tingle. And I will stretch over Jerusalem the line of Samaria and the plummet of the house of Ahab, and I will wipe Jerusalem as one wipes a dish, wiping it and turning it upside down. And I will abandon the remnant of My inheritance and deliver them into the hand of their enemies, and they will become as plunder and spoil to all their enemies; because they have done evil in My sight, and have been pro-*

voking Me to anger, since the day their fathers came from Egypt, even to this day.'" MOREOVER, MANASSEH SHED VERY MUCH INNOCENT BLOOD UNTIL HE HAD FILLED JERUSALEM FROM ONE END TO ANOTHER.

2 Kings 21:10-16a

King Manasseh was charged with both practicing and making those under him to practice every sort of demonic activity, along with shedding innocent blood, *"until he had filled Jerusalem from one end to another."* So now we can understand the magnitude of the darkness of this leader.

We gain a glimpse of Manasseh's wickedness when we see that in this case God did something almost unheard of in the Scriptures: He lowered the standard by which He would judge Manasseh and Judah:

" *'And I will stretch over Jerusalem the line of Samaria and the plummet of the house of Ahab....'"* 2 Kings 21:13a

God would use the standard of the wicked King Ahab, who had brought guilt upon Israel in great measure in previous days. The Northern Kingdom of Israel bore the fruit of wicked monarchy throughout its existence as a separate nation from the Southern Kingdom of Judah; yet God would compare and judge the vile leadership of King Manasseh against the standard of one of Israel's most wicked kings. Even by that standard, Manasseh still could not measure up. (See 1 Kings 16:29 through chapter 22 to learn about King Ahab.)

Promised Joy, Promised Judgment

We must understand how low God was setting the bar in order to try to show mercy to Jerusalem. If He had made His own righteousness the standard, and not that of Ahab and Samaria, Jerusalem would have had a worse end than Sodom and Gomorrah. It would not even exist as a city today if His own character had been His criterion for judging Manasseh and Judah.

Consequently, could there still be something, anything at all, in the infinity of a just and holy God to render mercy to such a leader?

> *Therefore the L*ORD *brought the commanders of the army of the king of Assyria against them, and they captured Manasseh with hooks, bound him with bronze chains, and took him to Babylon. And when he was in distress, he entreated the L*ORD *his God and humbled himself greatly before the God of his fathers. WHEN HE PRAYED TO HIM, HE WAS MOVED BY HIS ENTREATY AND HEARD HIS SUPPLICATION, AND BROUGHT HIM AGAIN TO JERUSALEM TO HIS KINGDOM. THEN MANASSEH KNEW THAT THE LORD WAS GOD.*
>
> 2 Chronicles 33:11-13

Although this most heinous of leaders incurred the absolute wrath of Almighty God against his nation, this same wicked man humbled himself enough to speak to the most deep-seated feeling in the heart of God …that of mercy. And when God poured out His mercy on this leader, King Manasseh *knew* that the Lord was God.

A Cry for Unrighteous Leaders

If such a man could pray for himself and have the ear of God, how much more can we as believers know we shall be heard when we cry out for our leaders. For then cities and nations would not have to be reduced to such pathetic conditions before acknowledging the God of the universe to gain needed tranquility and quietness.

Nine

Faith for Justice

> *"...now shall not God bring about justice for His elect, who cry to Him day and night.... However, when the Son of Man comes, will He find* [the] *faith on the earth?"*   Luke 18:7a, 8b

We have already established that God's nature demands justice. When a person believes in God through the work of Jesus on the cross, he is born again, taking on the new nature of the Parent, God the Father (see 1 Peter 1:23; 2 Peter 1:2-7). We have known that we are to be like God in our nature; that is, in love, joy, peace, patience, kindness, goodness, faithfulness, gentleness and self-control (see Galatians 5:22).

But have you considered that we also have within us His nature of justice, even as Adam and his wife had it before they disobeyed God in the garden? God had to reintroduce and re-establish this characteristic in the nature of man. He did this through His Son, Jesus, while Jesus walked on the earth as a man. We are to be like Jesus in our rebirthed nature. Thus we are to have His attitude concerning justice.

> *But of the Son He says…* "THOU HAST LOVED RIGHTEOUSNESS AND HATED LAWLESSNESS; THEREFORE GOD, THY GOD, HATH ANOINTED THEE WITH THE OIL OF GLADNESS ABOVE THY COMPANIONS." Hebrews 1:8a, 9

The writer of Hebrews was describing the nature of the Son of God, quoting from Psalm 45:7. The word *"righteousness"* here is the same word translated *"justice"* in that Psalm. Jesus both loved justice and hated lawlessness, the opposite of justice. When we come into the presence of Almighty God, such as in prayer or worship, we cannot help but notice His holiness. That holiness is the root for a love of justice and a hatred for that which tears down justice. We are partakers of that nature of holiness, as Peter said in his second epistle. Thus we are to be like Jesus, loving justice *and* hating injustice—which is lawlessness.

God is looking for this nature in His people. We must understand that this is an interwoven cord of both loving justice and hating lawlessness. This aspect of God's nature is not divided. It is a single attribute of His nature. It can be too easy for us to hate lawlessness without equally loving righteousness, which can result in an attitude of disliking people, not really caring whether or not they fall under judgment. We must understand that this dual characteristic of God will be a necessity in the last days if we are to maintain our relationship with God.

> *"And because lawlessness is increased, most people's love will grow cold. But the one who endures*

to the end, he shall be saved."

Matthew 24:12-13

We will need to cry out for justice in the last days. As a matter of fact, the opening Scripture text of this chapter tells us that Jesus will be looking for this faith for justice when He returns. Jesus was teaching us and encouraging us to have this kind of faith because His Father is anxious to answer those whose hearts long for justice.

Christ once told a parable to encourage His followers to believe without losing heart:

"There was in a certain city a judge who did not fear God, and did not respect man. And there was a widow in that city, and she kept coming to him, saying, 'Give me legal protection from my opponent.' And for a while he was unwilling; but afterward he said to himself, 'Even though I do not fear God nor respect man, yet because this widow bothers me, I will give her legal protection, lest by continually coming she wear me out.' " And the Lord said, "Hear what the unrighteous judge said; now shall not God bring about justice for His elect, who cry to Him day and night, and will He delay long over them? I tell you that He will bring about justice for them speedily. However, when the Son of Man comes, will He find [the] *faith on the earth?"*

Luke 18:2-8

Jesus was teaching about persevering in prayer, with an emphasis on crying out for justice. Does this seem strange? Yet, this is what praying for the Kingdom of God on earth is to be. This is how we are to pray. A kingdom is a dominion based on the justice system of that kingdom's ruler. You either agree with the rule of that leader or you don't. If you yearn for the Kingdom of God, you must desire His justice system.

Who is your opponent on earth? From whom do you need God's justice to protect you? Who is the one that wars against your faith to tear you down, to bring misery, to keep someone from believing in Jesus as the Savior, or to keep your city in a place of functional tolerance so as not to turn to God? It is time, beloved, for the justice of God to come with the power and the authority of Heaven. It is time for the Stronger Man to come with the justice purchased for mankind at the cross, a justice that swiftly exposes the defeat of the strong man who has mocked believers for holding onto a good confession of faith. But we must have the kind of faith that "dogs" *the* Judge until *His* justice prevails. I do not say this irreverently. God is looking for this bulldog type of faith—a faith that does not let go in crying out to Him until justice is served.

> *For our struggle is not against flesh and blood, but against the rulers, against the powers, against the world forces of this darkness, against the spiritual forces of wickedness in the heavenly places. …With all prayer and petition pray at all times in the Spirit, and with this in view, be on the alert with all perseverance and petition for all the saints.* Ephesians 6:12, 18

It is time, beloved, for vindication from the accusations and assaults of the opponent of men's souls. Faith for justice does not require that *we ourselves* be the strong man, standing in our own strength against the devil. Instead, faith for justice requires that we knock and knock and knock until *God* judges with a ruling that puts a halt to the enemy's ability to mock and intimidate without retribution. God has given believers authority by His Spirit to see His Kingdom's rule actively enforced in our daily lives (see Matthew 16:16-19).

The book of Acts records how the Church of that time cried out for justice in order to be able to continue to take in the harvest of souls. Peter and John had been used by Jesus to heal a paralytic, a man who was carried day after day to sit at the entrance to the Temple. There he spent his days begging for help from those who passed by.

Now, this miracle was not done in secret. All who had come to the Temple throughout the past several decades had seen this man by the Temple gates. When they suddenly saw him walking, it was obvious that something awesome had occurred. The Sadducees, along with the high priest, became jealous of Peter and John—as though the two apostles had been looking for fame—and had them arrested. After they were brought before the council of the elders, they were threatened and ordered not to preach in the name of Jesus anymore. Peter and John replied that they had to obey God rather than man, and so they would continue to preach. The Sadducees threatened them again and let them go.

Peter and John did not arrogantly walk out and immediately begin to preach again. They understood that this was a spiritual issue to intimidate them into quitting their work of evangelism. The Kingdom of God was being challenged...and so they took the issue to their King. They saw that the issues were souls and eternity, not apostles against Sadducees.

> *And when they had been released, they went to their own companions and reported all that the chief priests and the elders had said to them. And when they heard this, they lifted their voices to God with one accord and said, "O Lord, it is Thou who DIDST MAKE THE HEAVEN AND THE EARTH AND THE SEA, AND ALL THAT IS IN THEM, who by the Holy Spirit, through the mouth of our father David Thy servant, didst say, 'WHY DID THE GENTILES RAGE, AND THE PEOPLES DEVISE FUTILE THINGS? THE KINGS OF THE EARTH TOOK THEIR STAND, AND THE RULERS WERE GATHERED TOGETHER AGAINST THE LORD, AND AGAINST HIS CHRIST.' For truly in this city there were gathered together against Thy holy servant Jesus, whom Thou didst anoint, both Herod and Pontius Pilate, along with the Gentiles and the peoples of Israel, to do whatever Thy hand and Thy purpose predestined to occur. And now, Lord, take note of their threats, and grant that Thy bond-servants may speak Thy word with all confidence, while Thou dost extend Thy hand to heal, and signs and wonders take place through the name of Thy holy servant Jesus." And when they had prayed, the place where they had gathered together was shaken, and they were all filled with the Holy Spirit, and began to speak the word of God with boldness.*
>
> Acts 4:23-31

Peter and John and the rest of the Church needed God to act on their behalf, lest the enemy prevail against them and their work be stalled. God poured out His justice, and His Word through His people advanced with boldness. It is not that the Church had no mercy on the Jewish leaders, but they realized that a number of those leaders would try to halt the advance of the message of the Gospel at any cost.

We cannot have hatred in our hearts for those who hinder the Gospel. Jesus instructed His followers to pray for their enemies, not against them (see Matthew 5:44). But we must also pray for the advancement of the Gospel, which sometimes requires God to move by justice. There can be only one of two outcomes for those who actively resist the advance of the Kingdom. They will either be converted to the Gospel message, as Saul was converted through his supernatural experience with Jesus while on his way to take believers to prison (see Acts 9), or they will be removed out of the way, as King Herod was after he'd had the Apostle James killed and then shortly afterward took glory from the crowds upon himself (see Acts 12).

Finally, to God belongs vengeance and vindication. And there are times when we will need both, lest the work of the Gospel and all that Jesus paid for on the cross be of none effect.

> *"When the Son of Man comes, will He find* [the justice-seeking kind of] *faith on earth?"*
> Luke 18:8b

Ten

For Such a Time as This: The Story of Esther

The account of Esther is, I believe, the clearest picture in Scripture of the joy of a renewed life, the judgment by an adversary to ruin lives, and the imperative responsibility upon those who are renewed to cry out for justice—all of this in other words: promised joy, promised judgment and a cry for the city. As I explained in the introduction, the Holy Spirit used the book of Esther to show me things about the renewal that came to the Church in the early 1990's. As that renewal continued, the Holy Spirit kept showing me where the Church was positioned in relation to this story.

Some readers may not understand the prophetic aspect of this story as it pertains to the renewal that swept the earth in the 1990's, because you may not have been aware of this move. But I encourage you to continue reading. It is important that we understand the stepping stones of God's purposes for what is to come based on moves of God in history.

Promised Joy, Promised Judgment

As we look at the story of Esther's life, my prayer is that you will clearly see the dire need for justice to bring about a deliverance for the masses of humanity doomed to a decree of death, especially for those who live in the cities of our nations. The majority of national populations dwell in cities. If the Church believes there is to be a great harvest of souls won to the Kingdom of God in the last days, then we must realize practically that the harvest must be reaped from the places wherein dwell the greatest number of souls — the cities. The account of Esther shows us what the justice of one king did to literally convert masses of people to a God they did not previously know.

> *Now it took place in the days of Ahasuerus* [also known as Xerxes], *the Ahasuerus who reigned from India to Ethiopia over 127 provinces, in those days as King Ahasuerus sat on his royal throne which was in Susa the capital, in the third year of his reign, he gave a banquet for all his princes and attendants, the army officers of Persia and Media, the nobles, and the princes of his provinces being in his presence. And he displayed the riches of his royal glory and the splendor of his great majesty for many days, 180 days. And when these days were completed, the king gave a banquet lasting seven days for all the people who were present in Susa the capital, from the greatest to the least, in the court of the garden of the king's palace.*   Esther 1:1-5

King Ahasuerus ruled a kingdom comprised of 127 provinces. Today most of those provinces are nations.

Indeed, many of the provinces had previously been nations. These were conquered by the Assyrians, then later by the Babylonians, before being taken over by the Medes and the Persians. Judah, Israel, Ethiopia and India were among these nations. The entire empire included much of the lower half of the continent of Asia.

Now, the purpose for King Ahasuerus' banquet was political: He wanted to convince the heads of a number of those provinces to join with him in a planned battle against the small but growing power of the Greeks in Europe. This banquet to win the favor of these provincial war lords lasted six months. At the end of the six months, the king was in such good spirits that he opened the banquet to all the people within the capital city, both prominent and peasant; and this city-wide banquet lasted seven days. The roots of the book of Esther lie in an incident that took place at the end of this six-month, seven-day feast.

From this point in history, the annals of earth and Heaven separate, for each realm viewed what was to follow from different perspectives. Earth's history books describe a military campaign that would eventually bear the fruit of failure; it was the beginning of the end of the Persian Empire. Within a century and a half, the empire of Persia would be totally lost to Alexander the Great of Macedonia; and that downfall began with this particular campaign.

Heaven's record, however, describes a marriage that fell apart, another that took place, and the deliverance of a people group that many have tried to annihilate over the centuries. This latter documentation is the line that we will follow. True justice from Heaven, after all, does not lie in the battles of the empires of the earth; rather, it is found in the battle between greater forces, one spiritual force attempting to do away with the plan and purpose of a Greater. For if the serpent of old could destroy this particular people, the fulfillment of the promise of the seed of the woman would never come to pass.

> *On the seventh day, when the heart of the king was merry with wine, he commanded Mehuman, Biztha, Harbona, Bigtha, Abagtha, Zethar, and Carkas, the seven eunuchs who served in the presence of King Ahasuerus, to bring Queen Vashti before the king with her royal crown in order to display her beauty to the people and the princes, for she was beautiful. But Queen Vashti refused to come at the king's command delivered by the eunuchs. Then the king became very angry and his wrath burned within him.*
>
> Esther 1:10-12

Vashti is a type, a symbol of the Church who walks in her own ways, disregarding the word of King Jesus. She is beautiful, because the work of the cross of Jesus, through His shed blood, has made her beautiful. But this beauty, when left to selfishness, turns into pride, with no desire to serve at the King's bidding. She no longer fears the King. And because of it, her conduct has been made known to all.

> *Charm is deceitful and beauty is vain, but a woman who fears the LORD, she shall be praised.*
> Proverbs 31:30

FOR SUCH A TIME AS THIS: THE STORY OF ESTHER

For "THE NAME OF GOD IS BLASPHEMED AMONG THE GENTILES BECAUSE OF YOU".... Romans 2:24

When the Church of Jesus, the Bride of Christ, walks in her own ways, she begins to look like the world. And then the world says, "Why do I need your Jesus? What's the difference between the way you act and the way I act?"

This may sound severe, but I truly believe that Jesus has cut off that Bride, the Vashti Church. In 1987, God allowed the exposure of several preachers caught in sin. Although this exposure began with those who oversaw nationally known ministries, the light of God was turned to shine down through the ranks. It was necessary, even though the world saw the Church's conduct and blasphemed the name of Jesus for it. But God was concerned both for the lost *and* for the Church who was letting the lost go to Hell with very little concern. How could the justice and lovingkindness of God win a world to Christ if they weren't enough to change the Church? But the justice of God *was* about to change the Church—so that He might also gain the lost! The Vashti Church was being judged.

> *Then the king said to the wise men who understood the times—for it was the custom of the king so to speak before all who knew law and justice..."According to law, what is to be done with Queen Vashti, because she did not obey the command of King Ahasuerus delivered by the eunuchs?"*
>
> *And in the presence of the king and the princes, Memucan said, "Queen Vashti has wronged not*

> *only the king but also all the princes, and all the peoples who are in all the provinces of King Ahasuerus. For the queen's conduct will become known to all....*
>
> *"If it pleases the king, let a royal edict be issued by him and let it be written in the laws of Persia and Media so that it cannot be repealed, that Vashti should come no more into the presence of King Ahasuerus, and let the king give her royal position to another who is more worthy than she."* Esther 1:13, 15, 16-17a, 19

Vashti was banished from the presence of the king.

> *For it is time for judgment to BEGIN WITH THE HOUSEHOLD OF GOD; and if it begins with us first, what will be the outcome for those who do not obey the gospel of God? AND IF IT IS WITH DIFFICULTY THAT THE RIGHTEOUS IS SAVED, WHAT WILL BECOME OF THE GODLESS MAN AND THE SINNER?*
> 1 Peter 4:17-18

It was time to look for a new Bride, one who would love Jesus and one who would fear God, so that her conduct could be made known to all...without regret. This new Bride would first have to come into the King's "palace," if you will, to soak in His anointing for a time, in order to be made to smell like royalty. She would also need to be dressed in the beauty of the King. This new Bride-to-be would have to come away for a time to go through this process. She would be hidden from the eyes of the world so that when she finally emerged, the eyes of the world would not be blinded by their familiarity with the old queen.

Thus came the outpouring of God's Holy Spirit in Toronto, Canada in 1994. Many would come from all over the earth to soak in the anointing there.

> *After these things when the anger of King Ahasuerus had subsided, he remembered Vashti and what she had done and what had been decreed against her. Then the king's attendants, who served him, said, "Let beautiful young virgins be sought for the king. And let the king appoint overseers in all the provinces of his kingdom that they may gather every beautiful young virgin to Susa the capital, to the harem, into the custody of Hegai, the king's eunuch, who is in charge of the women; and let their cosmetics be given them. Then let the young lady who pleases the king be queen in place of Vashti." And the matter pleased the king, and he did accordingly.*
>
> Esther 2:1-4

Among those brought to the palace was an orphaned young lady named Esther who was being raised by her cousin Mordecai. When she was taken to the palace, her cousin gave her strict instructions not to make her people known—that is, she was not to let the people at the palace know that she was Jewish. Thus Esther was brought to the palace, one of a number of young virgins from the provinces (the nations).

> *Now when the turn of each young lady came to go in to King Ahasuerus, AFTER THE END OF HER TWELVE MONTHS UNDER THE REGULA-*

Promised Joy, Promised Judgment

TIONS FOR THE WOMEN—FOR THE DAYS OF THEIR BEAUTIFICATION WERE COMPLETED AS FOLLOWS: SIX MONTHS WITH OIL OF MYRRH AND SIX MONTHS WITH SPICES AND THE COSMETICS FOR WOMEN...

Esther 2:12

Esther "soaked" in the king's fragrances for one year. Not only was she beautiful, but the favor of the Lord was upon her. And the king loved her. Esther became the king's choice to replace Vashti as queen.

But look at the timetable according to Scripture: The original banquet was given in the third year of King Ahasuerus' reign (see Esther 1:3), and Esther was chosen after her twelve months' preparation time, at the end of the king's seventh year (see Esther 2:16). Esther did not become queen until almost four years after Vashti had been removed from her royal position.

Thus it was with the present situation which began in Toronto, Ontario, Canada, in 1994. It appeared that the Bride of Christ was "soaking" in the anointing of the oil and fragrances of the Holy Spirit for several years, until about 1997. That is not to say that what was taking place suddenly came to a halt. Rather, there was a change in the "coming away out of the world," so to speak, to a place of being chosen as the one who looked as though royalty was now upon her. That time period disturbed many believers who felt that the world was not being affected, but that those who were partaking in this move were just being selfish. However, this was a strategic, divine, set-apart time of God's making.

After King Ahasuerus chose Esther to be his queen, a man named Haman was promoted to the highest position in the kingdom, above all the counselors and princes of the king. Haman was an Agagite (Esther 3:1), by authority of rank in his native roots. We have to travel back hundreds of years before the time of Esther to understand the meaning of the term *Agagite*. The Agagites were descendants of royalty, kings of the Amalekites, known by title as *Agag*. This was similar to the title of *Pharaoh* for Egyptians or *Caesar* for the Romans. Amalek, the father of the Amalekites, was the grandson of Esau, a son of Esau's son's concubine (see Genesis 36:12). This is significant because, as Esau was a godless man (see Hebrews 12:16) and antagonistic toward his brother Jacob (see Genesis 27:41), so his descendants were identical in nature toward the sons of Israel, the descendants of Jacob.

This unprovoked antagonism in the Amalekites became apparent when the Hebrews were coming out of Egyptian slavery to enter the Promised Land of Canaan. For no known reason, the Amalekites attacked the weary ex-slaves to destroy them (see Exodus 17). Amalek did not win the overall battle; but neither were they utterly destroyed themselves. However, because of this provocation, God swore to destroy them:

> *Then the L*ORD *said to Moses, "Write this in a book as a memorial and recite it to Joshua, that I will utterly blot out the memory of Amalek from under heaven."* Exodus 17:14

God later instructed Moses that after the Israelites had taken the Promised Land and they had peace all around them, they were to go forth and destroy the Amalekites (see Deuteronomy 25:19). Several genera-

Promised Joy, Promised Judgment

tions passed. Saul, the first king of Israel, was commanded by the Lord through the prophet Samuel to destroy all the Amalekites (see 1 Samuel 15:1-3). Saul killed them all...all except for Agag, the royalty of Amalek (see 1 Samuel 15:9). And so the hatred of the Israelites would continue in the royal line of Amalek for several more centuries...until we reach the story of Esther. But the disregard by God toward Amalek was likewise continued, through the person of Mordecai.

> *And all the king's servants who were at the king's gate bowed down and paid homage to Haman; for so the king had commanded concerning him. But Mordecai neither bowed down nor paid homage. Then the king's servants who were at the king's gate said to Mordecai, "Why are you transgressing the king's command?" Now it was when they had spoken daily to him and he would not listen to them, that they told Haman to see whether Mordecai's reason would stand; for he had told them that he was a Jew. When Haman saw that Mordecai neither bowed down nor paid homage to him, Haman was filled with rage. But he disdained to lay hands on Mordecai alone, for they had told him who the people of Mordecai were; therefore Haman sought to destroy all the Jews, the people of Mordecai, who were throughout the whole kingdom of Ahasuerus.*
>
> Esther 3:2-6

Haman is a type of Satan. Satan's goal is to destroy not just one life, but entire nations. Like Haman, Satan does have princely power; and like Haman, Satan schemes in order to bring about misery and destruction (see Ephesians 2:2, 6:11; John 10:10).

Haman went to King Ahasuerus with a most cunning, sly, deceitful request.

> *Then Haman said to King Ahasuerus, "There is a certain people scattered and dispersed among the peoples in all the provinces of your kingdom; their laws are different from those of all other people and they do not observe the king's laws, so it is not in the king's interest to let them remain. If it is pleasing to the king, let it be decreed that they be destroyed, and I will pay ten thousand talents of silver into the hands of those who carry on the king's business, to put into the king's treasuries."*
>
> *Then the king took his signet ring from his hand and gave it to Haman, the son of Hammedatha the Agagite, the enemy of the Jews. And the king said to Haman, "The silver is yours, and the people also, to do with them as you please."*
>
> Esther 3:8-11

Read that request of Haman again. He intentionally did not mention an important piece of information. Do you see what it is? I'll reveal this toward the end of the chapter.

> *Then the king's scribes were summoned on the thirteenth day of the first month, and it was written just as Haman commanded to the king's satraps, to the governors who were over each province, and to the princes of each people, each province according to its script, each people according to its language, being written in the*

name of King Ahasuerus and sealed with the king's signet ring. And letters were sent by couriers to all the king's provinces to destroy, to kill, and to annihilate all the Jews, both young and old, women and children, in one day, the thirteenth day of the twelfth month, which is the month of Adar, and to seize their possessions as plunder. A copy of the edict to be issued as law in every province was published to all the peoples so that they should be ready for this day. The couriers went out compelled by the king's command while the decree was issued in Susa the capital; and while the king and Haman sat down to drink, the city of Susa was in confusion.

Esther 3:12-15

A death decree was issued and would take effect throughout the kingdom of Ahasuerus exactly twelve months from the time Haman had this decree written down. All the Jews were to be annihilated, with their goods going as plunder to those who killed them. And all the while there was confusion in the city where Haman lived, there was drinking in the palace. Do you see the prophetic picture? The devil is quite happy if he can ensure the deaths of people groups, especially in the cities of nations. And all the while, he makes sure there is confusion in the streets until the decree of death is carried out.

The palace is a picture of the Church inside her four walls, untouched by those going to Hell. But God has some who are His—and who do not dwell in the palace. They don't seem to have the authority to bring about the major citywide changes that are necessary;

but they know some who are inside the palace. Those who dwell outside the palace know those within who need to hear the cries of the ones destined to die, who can make a difference through strategic intercession, if they will only be touched by the feelings of those on the streets of their city. There is a new Bride in the palace who has won the intimate heart of her husband, the King of all the kingdoms of the earth—of nations and cities.

> *When Mordecai learned all that had been done, he tore his clothes, put on sackcloth and ashes, and went out into the midst of the city and wailed loudly and bitterly. And he went as far as the king's gate, for no one was to enter the king's gate clothed in sackcloth. And in each and every province where the command and decree of the king came, there was great mourning among the Jews, with fasting, weeping, and wailing; and many lay on sackcloth and ashes.* Esther 4:1-3

Mordecai immediately realized the severity of the decree, although it was not to be carried out for an entire year. Some might say, "Of course he would take it seriously. What else would he do?" But I say to you, "A decree of death has been issued today—the devil's. Do you take it seriously?"

> *Then Esther's maidens and her eunuchs came and told her, and the queen writhed in great anguish. And she sent garments to clothe Mordecai that he might remove his sackcloth from him, but he did not accept them. Then Esther summoned*

Promised Joy, Promised Judgment

Hathach from the king's eunuchs, whom the king had appointed to attend her, and ordered him to go to Mordecai to learn what this was and why it was. So Hathach went out to Mordecai to the city square in front of the king's gate. And Mordecai told him all that had happened to him, and the exact amount of money that Haman had promised to pay to the king's treasuries for the destruction of the Jews. He also gave him a copy of the text of the edict which had been issued in Susa for their destruction, that he might show Esther and inform her, and to order her to go to the king to implore his favor and to plead with him for her people. And Hathach came back and related Mordecai's words to Esther. Esther 4:4-9

Esther, a type of the Church that experienced the renewal of the early 1990's, was in the palace, enjoying the goodness of the king. She did not hear the cries of those under the sentence of the decree. She did not understand the heart of her own family member who had chosen not to sit with her inside, but rather to remain among those who would die. There is an intentional prophetic slant here. Do you see the correlation to the Church? Do you hear what God is saying?

Esther was told by her maids that something was wrong; yet it seems that they did not tell her specifically of the decree itself. All she seems to know at this point in the account is that her cousin is wearing sackcloth and ashes at the king's gate, and that he therefore is not coming inside the palace gate. Instead of finding out why Mordecai is dressed that way, she merely sends new clothes so that he can come inside the king's gates as before. Mordecai is not moved in any way whatsoever by Esther's newfound royalty—not because he is arrogant, but because he sees a possible higher purpose for her royalty which he realizes has yet to take hold in her heart. The reason for her coming into royalty has not yet been grasped by her; she has taken for granted both her choosing and her status.

After Mordecai refuses Esther's kindness, she sends one of the king's eunuchs to ask why he refused the garments. Mordecai succinctly gives his reason and sends the eunuch back with a copy of the edict and a commission to speak to the king.

> *Then Esther spoke to Hathach and ordered him to reply to Mordecai: "All the king's servants and the people of the king's provinces know that for any man or woman who comes to the king to the inner court who is not summoned, he has but one law, that he be put to death, unless the king holds out to him the golden scepter so that he may live. And I have not been summoned to come to the king for these thirty days."* Esther 4:10-13

Even after hearing Mordecai's account, Esther still did not perceive her destiny as the queen of the largest empire then on the earth. She was still enjoying the goodness of the palace life and realized that she herself could be put to death if she breached royal etiquette. She was thinking primarily of self, not of the many untold numbers whose lives would be lost if she did not act. Esther sent word back to Mordecai that she had not been summoned to come into the king's presence in a month.

Promised Joy, Promised Judgment

Let the reader hear: Esther had known this king intimately as her husband, but she had not yet known him for who he was—a king who sat on the throne for justice. She had known him in the bedroom, but not in the throne room. And she feared the place she had not yet entered. Make no mistake, the throne room *is* a fearful place. It is the place where evil is judged. It is the place of justice and judgment decreed and carried out.

> *But the* Lord *abides forever; HE HAS ESTABLISHED HIS THRONE FOR JUDGMENT.*
> Psalm 9:7

> *A king who sits on the throne of justice disperses all evil with his eyes.* Proverbs 20:8

> *God is a righteous judge, and a God who has indignation every day.* Psalm 7:11

The seriousness of the matter moved Mordecai to respond immediately to the queen:

> *Then Mordecai told them to reply to Esther, "Do not imagine that you in the king's palace can escape any more than all the Jews. For if you remain silent at this time, relief and deliverance will arise for the Jews from another place and you and your father's house will perish. AND WHO KNOWS WHETHER YOU HAVE NOT ATTAINED ROYALTY FOR SUCH A TIME AS THIS?"*
> Esther 4:13-14

Mordecai did not answer her with a rebuke, but with

earnestness and sobriety, impressing upon Esther that she also would perish with the outside world. If she chose to maintain her silence, another deliverer would be raised up in her place. Mordecai finished his words to her by causing her to see the divine purpose for the path of destiny into which she had been placed.

I believe the Lord would say to the Church, "You have been made into royalty (see Revelation 5:10), you who were nothing in status before the Almighty (see 1 Peter 1:24). *Perhaps you have attained this royalty for such a time as this!*"

Esther had to allow these grave words of her father-hearted cousin to sink deeply into her soul. She had to understand the consequences of her obedience to Mordecai's request to herself and family, as well as to the multitudes who lived in the cities all over the kingdom.

As her cousin's words penetrated her soul, Esther finally understood her responsibility. She sent a message to him with one final thought...

> *"...And thus I will go in to the king, which is not according to the law; and if I perish, I perish."*
> Esther 4:16

Jesus' words are appropriate here:

> *"For whoever wishes to save his life shall lose it; but whoever loses his life for My sake and the gospel's shall save it."* Mark 8:35

Jesus would fulfill His own words as He set the example of One who gave up His royalty for the sake of those who were doomed to die.

When Esther had been selected queen, King Ahasuerus had held a banquet for her because of his love for her and the joy that she brought to him (see Esther 2:18). Now, five years later, the tables were about to be turned. Esther was about to give a banquet for the king. Still, she would first have to go into that fearful place—the throne room—to invite him. Esther set herself and her maidens to fast for three days, and she asked Mordecai to do the same.

> *Now it came about on the third day that ESTHER PUT ON HER ROYAL ROBES and stood in the inner court of the king's palace in front of the king's rooms, and the king was sitting on his royal throne in the throne room, opposite the entrance to the palace. And it happened when the king saw Esther the queen standing in the court, she obtained favor in his sight; and the king extended to Esther the golden scepter which was in his hand. So Esther came near and touched the top of the scepter.* Esther 5:1-2

Esther was quite unlike Vashti. This queen was humble, and she had regard for the king. Her attitude of deference spoke volumes to King Ahasuerus, who loved this queen of his whom he had not seen in several weeks. Esther had done well in preparing her heart as she realized that her husband was also a man of justice, a king who had all the authority needed to carry out the law of the kingdom in righteousness. If she had been like the beautiful but arrogant Vashti, she would have lost her head.

Something else stands out strongly in her entrance into the throne room: Esther was a *queen*...not a beggar. She sought justice against one who was powerful. And she would use her royal position to gain it. Esther was walking in skillful wisdom and prudence. She had thought through her strategy. She'd had to. Hers was no easy task. Remember from chapter 1:19 that the laws of the Medes and Persians, which were branded with the king's signet, could *not* be changed. Furthermore, Haman was a skillfully deceitful man who just happened to have the highest favor in the land with the king.

Thus Esther gained the initial favor needed, as King Ahasuerus, her husband, extended to her the golden scepter (because she had won his heart years earlier). And he readily accepted her invitation to the banquet she had prepared.

Queen Esther gave her banquet for two men: her husband-king, and Haman. At this banquet she did not immediately assault with words this enemy of her people who sat there drinking with the king and queen. When the king asked her the reason for the banquet, she responded only by inviting him and Haman to another banquet the following night.

This is intriguing. She knew something, I think, about the king, her husband, something that Haman and others were not so quick to perceive. The king was an inquisitive man, a man who desired understanding unto wisdom, a man who continually sought to know truth. This king knew the meekness of his queen. I believe he understood clearly that something was troubling her, although she had as yet said nothing of the matter. He knew this because he, more than anyone, understood that Esther had put her life on the line when she came into the throne room of justice. And he knew that she had done so for a more pressing reason than merely issuing an invitation to a banquet. She could simply have sent word through a messenger if that had been her sole purpose.

Esther did not reveal her heart's request to her king that first night. Yet she had awakened in her husband a thirst to search for something. He did not yet know what it was…but something was not properly in order in the halls of his palace or, indeed, somewhere in the expanse of his kingdom.

It is the glory of God to conceal a matter, but the glory of kings is to search out a matter.
Proverbs 25:2

The day had been long. The banquet was finished, and Haman was going home. On the way he had to pass by the sackcloth-draped man he so hated. This brought a bitter end to so sweet a night for Haman.

But the king's adrenaline was beginning to flow. His eyes would not shut this night.

During that night the king could not sleep so he gave an order to bring the book of records, the chronicles, and they were read before the king. And it was found written what Mordecai had reported concerning Bigthana and Teresh, two of the king's eunuchs who were doorkeepers, that they had sought to lay hands on King Ahasuerus.
Esther 6:1-2

These two verses flow past the eye so quickly that it is easy to miss the fact that the reading of the records literally took all night—hours and hours. The king's exhausted attendants had to stand erect throughout the night as they read and read and read from the history books of this king's reign.

As the king sat on his throne listening, the constellations in the night sky slowly made their trek across their destined paths. Their light gradually began to fade as the sun's light barely broke across the eastern sky. The attendants who read the records were reading about the seventh year of his reign when suddenly the king interrupted.

He recalled this incident, the plot to assassinate him. It had been discovered and reported by a Jew named Mordecai. These very words being read to him had been written in his presence five years before, as the two eunuchs were hanging on the gallows (see Esther 2:21-23). Such loyalty by a subject of his kingdom had caused his life to be spared. Any king would desire such loyalty. And now, almost five years later, the king was wondering aloud if such allegiance had been rewarded.

> *And the king said, "What honor or dignity has been bestowed on Mordecai for this?"*
> *Then the king's servants who attended him said, "Nothing has been done for him."* Esther 6:3

The character of the king was such that he could not let Mordecai's actions on his behalf pass unnoticed, even half a decade afterward. Besides, if the king were to honor such loyalty before the eyes of all his people, would it not engender more loyalty among his subjects? After all, who wouldn't want to be honored by the king?

Promised Joy, Promised Judgment

But how was the king to honor Mordecai? As he pondered this while the sun's rays were breaking over the horizon, he suddenly heard a noise in the courtyard, just outside the throne room.

> *So the king said, "Who is in the court?" Now Haman had just entered the outer court of the king's palace in order to speak to the king about hanging Mordecai on the gallows which he had prepared for him.*
>
> *The king's servants said to him, "Behold, Haman is standing in the court."*
>
> *And the king said, "Let him come in." So Haman came in and the king said to him, "What is to be done for the man whom the king desires to honor?"*
>
> *And Haman said to himself, "Whom would the king desire to honor more than me?"*
>
> Esther 6:4-6

Haman had been serving as one of the king's advisors for some time. Ahasuerus had given him the most exalted position over all of the other princes. And now the king wanted to know how to best honor someone! Haman's time had truly come!

There is quite a bit of irony in this incident. Did you discover what the important piece of information was that Haman had left out when he had come to the king with his proposition? He sought to annihilate "*a certain people*" from the kingdom because "*it is not in the king's interest to let them remain*" (Esther 3:8-9). Haman never mentioned to the king WHO THIS PEOPLE GROUP WAS! And although the decree clearly stated who they were, the king had given Haman his signet ring. Haman wrote the law in the name of King Ahasuerus, and so the king had not even seen the decree with his own eyes because he had trusted Haman with his signature. And now the king is doing the very same thing to Haman. The king did not mention the name of the *"certain person"* whom he wanted to honor. Haman was puffed up with his own pride. After all, the king had given him the highest position in the kingdom next only to the king; Queen Esther had just given a banquet for the king and him alone; and he was, that very day, invited as the lone guest to a second banquet with the king and queen. To whom could the king possibly be referring other than him?

So Haman set his mind to determine the most lavish deeds that could be done in the public's eye to bring to himself the most glory. And that would surely show those Jews—especially that one sitting outside the king's gate who never stood to honor him! It would also hopefully justify his request to hang Mordecai.

Haman thrust out his chest, smiled, and gave a most bloated suggestion. Afterward, he thought, he could request permission to rid the king's gate of that sackcloth-clad loser.

> *Then Haman said to the king, "For the man whom the king desires to honor, let them bring a royal robe which the king has worn, and the horse on which the king has ridden, and on whose head a royal crown has been placed; and let the robe and the horse be handed over to one of the king's most noble princes and let them array the man whom the king desires to honor and lead him on*

> *horseback through the city square, and proclaim before him, 'Thus it shall be done to the man whom the king desires to honor.'"*
>
> Esther 6:7-9

Haman paused to allow the king to reply, but King Ahasuerus had just one important issue on his mind. He had no idea that Haman had come to the palace to speak with him about hanging Mordecai; frankly, he wasn't at all interested in anything else that Haman might want to say. The king had been awake all night listening to the historical records of his first seven years of reigning. His attention had been jolted at the end of that long night of lost sleep by this issue of a commoner whom he had not rewarded for saving his life half a decade earlier. Ahasuerus would not let the sun go down on another day without taking care of this terribly belated matter.

Haman could barely breathe, so caught up was he in anticipation. He was about to get the shock of his life. *The very detail that each man hid from the other would be revealed that very day!* The first shock would hit Haman in less than a second. The second would have to wait until nightfall.

> *Then the king said to Haman, "Take quickly the robes and the horse as you have said, and do so for Mordecai the Jew, who is sitting at the king's gate; do not fall short in anything of all that you have said."*
>
> *So Haman took the robe and the horse, and arrayed Mordecai, and led him on horseback*

through the city square, and proclaimed before him, "Thus it shall be done to the man whom the king desires to honor." Then Mordecai returned to the king's gate. But Haman hurried home, mourning, with his head covered.

Esther 6:10-12

It is ironic that Mordecai had rebelled against the king's own edict and did not honor Haman by bowing down to him (see Esther 3:2). Yet Haman was ordered to completely fulfill the command of King Ahasuerus without falling short in any of it.

I'm sure Mordecai was honored in his heart that the king would do such for him, but he was not flattered or puffed up. The decree of death was still present. Mordecai did not forget this in the glory of the moment. And he also did not overstep his bounds. He did not come inside afterward to speak to the king, although he probably could have done so with the king's favor. Speaking with the king was still Queen Esther's task, and she was in the midst of walking out that responsibility.

Meanwhile Haman went home in shame, covering his head, which itself was prophetic.

And all of this had been put into motion because of Esther's first banquet!

Haman had yet to finish groaning to his wife and friends concerning the day's events when the king's eunuchs arrived to whisk him away to the queen's second banquet. Haman realized that he could not show his trouble in the presence of King Ahasuerus. He would have to try to go along with whatever the king wanted to talk about, being careful not to mention the gallows he had just had made for Mordecai back at his own house. Mordecai would still die in the annihilation of the Jews at the end of the year. But the eunuchs who had come to his house to bring him to the banquet had noticed the gallows.

This second night was Esther's night. She knew she had the full attention, heart and soul, of her husband, the king. He knew she had a request she wanted him to fulfill. And he would not let her go another night without letting him know that request. This king of justice was wrapped up with love for this wife of his who so honored him that he would offer her up to half of his kingdom. Follow the emotion that unfolds with this second banquet.

> *And the king said to Esther on the second day also as they drank their wine at the banquet, "What is your petition, Queen Esther? It shall be granted you. And what is your request? Even to half of the kingdom it shall be done."*
>
> *Then Queen Esther answered and said, "If I have found favor in your sight, O king, and if it pleases the king, let my life be given me as my petition, and my people as my request; for we have been sold, I and my people, to be destroyed, to be killed and to be annihilated. Now if we had only been sold as slaves, men and women, I would have remained silent, for the trouble would not be commensurate with the annoyance to the king."*
>
> *Then King Ahasuerus asked Queen Esther, "Who is he, and where is he, who would presume to do thus?"*
>
> *Esther said, "A foe and an enemy, is this wicked*

> *Haman!" Then Haman became terrified before the king and queen.*   Esther 7:2-6

I believe the king expected Queen Esther's answer to be somewhat serious, for she had risked her life when she came into the throne room the previous day to request his presence at her banquet. But I do not believe he anticipated the full gravity of her words. She knew she had his utmost attention and favor. He had extended his scepter to her to let her know this. And this game that Haman had played in not letting the king know who the "*certain people*" were that were of no interest to him had certainly backfired. This woman who had been chosen, this queen who was granted favor in the throne room of justice, along with that sackcloth-draped man sitting outside the king's gate who had saved the king's life years before — certainly they were both of utmost interest to the king.

Haman had covered his face earlier that day, after having led Mordecai around the city square and proclaimed the king's honor over him. Now he was about to have his face covered again…for the last time.

> *And the king arose in his anger from drinking wine and went into the palace garden; but Haman stayed to beg for his life from Queen Esther, for he saw that harm had been determined against him by the king. Now when the king returned from the palace garden into the place where they were drinking wine, Haman was falling on the couch where Esther was.*
>
> *Then the king said, "Will he even assault the queen with me in the house?" As the word went*

> *out of the king's mouth, they covered Haman's face.*
>
> *Then Harbonah, one of the eunuchs who were before the king said, "Behold indeed, the gallows standing at Haman's house fifty cubits high, which Haman made for Mordecai who spoke good on behalf of the king!"*
>
> *And the king said, "Hang him on it." So they hanged Haman on the gallows which he had prepared for Mordecai, and the king's anger subsided.* Esther 7:7-10

As much of a victory as this was, the battle was not yet over. The story could not end here. Why not? It could not end because the laws of the Medes and Persians could not be revoked. The writer of the decree had been judged, but the law which he had written was still in effect. *Esther's job had not yet been completed.* This is not to imply any failure whatsoever. But small victories can be misconstrued as complete victories, and rejoicing can easily come too quickly. If that were allowed to happen, the enemy would still win in the end.

Esther had put her life on the line, yet not for herself alone. If she had done this for herself, she would never have carried out the plan that she did. She had obtained a judgment against the enemy. But she still needed justice for a people who were to be annihilated because of the sly scheme devised against them.

King Ahasuerus thought that Esther had accomplished her goal. So he was probably surprised to find her again coming through the doors to the throne room.

> *Then Esther spoke again to the king, fell at his*

> *feet, wept, and implored him to avert the evil scheme of Haman the Agagite and his plot which he had devised against the Jews. ... Then she said, "If it pleases the king and if I have found favor before him and the matter seems proper to the king and I am pleasing in his sight, let it be written to revoke the letters devised by Haman, the son of Hammedatha the Agagite, which he wrote to destroy the Jews who are in all the king's provinces. For how can I endure to see the calamity which shall befall my people, and how can I endure to see the destruction of my kindred?"*
>
> Esther 8:3, 5-6

Esther apparently did not know that the laws of the Medes and the Persians could not be revoked. But she did understand that if something was not done by the king to give her people justice, she would watch as her people were ruthlessly destroyed. Esther needed the impossible from the throne room.

The most important issue concerning Esther's character here is her change in attitude. She has now identified herself, in her desperate plea before the king, with those doomed to death. She is honestly concerned for her people outside the palace. She is crying out in the place where they could not stand. She is pleading for what they could not.

Esther would win continued favor from her husband. Mordecai was then brought alongside in that favor, as Esther made known to King Ahasuerus Mordecai's relationship to her. The king gave Mordecai his signet ring, which he had taken back from Haman when he pronounced judgment on him. And although the original decree of Haman could not be revoked, divine wisdom came to Mordecai to write another law, sealed with the king's signet, that would give the Jews the right to defend themselves entirely against the mobs that were legally put together because of that first decree. We can read of this second decree in chapter eight of Esther.

We must look at the climax of Esther's efforts. We must see this, for in it lies the ultimate goal of the Church because it is the ultimate goal of Father God, put into motion when He sent His Son Jesus to effect a new decree, a new covenant, to override the old decree of death hanging over the masses. Look at the result of the second decree written by Mordecai.

> *And in each and every province, and in each and every city, wherever the king's commandment and his decree arrived, there was gladness and joy for the Jews, a feast and a holiday. AND MANY AMONG THE PEOPLES OF THE LAND BECAME JEWS, for the dread of the Jews had fallen on them.* Esther 8:17

The ultimate outcome of Esther's laying down her life to gain justice for her people was this: *The nations who were not her people BECAME HER PEOPLE,* for they converted to believe in the same way as the one who used her royalty…for such a time as this.

Eleven

The Spirit and the Bride Say, "Come"...to Whom?

And the Spirit and the bride say, "Come." And let the one who hears say, "Come." And let the one who is thirsty come; let the one who wishes take the water of life without cost.

Revelation 22:17

The title of this chapter asks a question that might be answered almost frivolously, if we don't look at the context of the verse from which the question arises, or if we do not understand the fullness of Jesus' desire for His Bride to long for Him. I initially intended to give an entirely different answer to the above question than the one which so quickly rolls from our lips; but the Holy Spirit keeps showing me that the one-word answer everyone would blurt out *is* the right answer—yet with a much fuller meaning than what is comprehended in so brief an answer.

It may seem strange to have this type of chapter in a

Promised Joy, Promised Judgment

book about judgment. Yet it is this God of justice who started life for man with a couple (see Genesis 1:27) and will end this age with a couple (see Revelation 19 and 21). Judgment was first begun with that first couple, and judgment on earth will end with the revelation of the second couple. The above scripture is found at the end of the New Testament. The judgment rendered at the cross and the judgments which are yet to take place, as seen in the book of Revelation, are tied together. The purpose of God through the Gospel of Christ contained in the entire New Testament is to win a Bride to Jesus through His redeeming work of judgment (see Revelation 5:9; 19:7-8).

We have already seen the relationship between a chosen bride and the need for justice in the story of Esther. The story is greatly magnified in these last days as the Bride of Christ, the Church, is in need of justice from the throne room in Heaven to be made manifest on earth for the salvation of cities throughout the nations.

The renewal that poured out so mightily through the Airport Vineyard Church in Toronto in 1994 reestablished the first-love relationship of the Church, which is the Bride of Christ, to Jesus our Lord. Several notable songs were birthed as a result of that first love, which brought about in the Church a longing for the return of Jesus, not for the sake of "getting out of here," but rather a pure, bridal longing to see the Bridegroom.

The verse from Revelation 22 quoted on the preceding page is a prophetic prayer of the Bride *and* the Holy Spirit, who is given to the Bride as a pledge of that promised wedding day (see Ephesians 1:13-14). As first love was again being established in the heart of the Bride of Christ, the heartbeat of Jesus the Bridegroom was also beginning to be heard. The renewal was the work of the Spirit of Jesus to woo the heart of the Bride back to the One to whom she is betrothed. Renewal was to bring the Bride to the place of longing for the heartbeat of Jesus. In other words, He won our hearts that we might in turn win His. He asked us to come back to Him that we might ask Him to come back to us. But, beloved, that pure longing for His return, according to the context of Revelation 22:17, is broader than we have conceived. Let us look at the verse again.

And the Spirit and the bride say, "Come." And let the one who hears say, "Come." And let the one who is thirsty come; let the one who wishes take the water of life without cost.

This is a call to Jesus *and* a call to the lost. This is the heartbeat of Jesus. This longing call for Jesus' return is seen as a type in the natural relationships which take place among us every day when a man and woman get engaged. The two here long to be married, knowing that together love will flourish and things will be accomplished in greater measure, and there will be children to birth.

I must confess that I have often prayed, "Lord, *don't* come back too soon, because I want to win more lost people to You. If You come back soon, it will be too late for those people." But the Holy Spirit in me keeps showing me that I am wrong in thinking this way. For this is a natural understanding of something that must be accomplished in the power and wisdom of the Spirit of Jesus. It is this kind of thinking that actually keeps some believers from praying for Jesus' soon return. The true longing and praying for His return is in direct correlation to seeing fulfillments of prophetic justice and judgments in order that the complete harvest of souls might finally be gathered in (see Revelation 14). This will complete the international Bride of Christ, with whom Jesus passionately longs to be. This is what the Holy Spirit is saying in Revelation 22:17.

Again, I saw this action—described as "soon coming equals more action"—in the natural relationship of an engaged couple, the woman being a type of the Church who *longs for* Jesus' return. The closer to the wedding day the bride-to-be gets, the more, and faster, the work for that day seems to be accomplished, because of the hope in her heart. The woman seems to have a more fervent heart in seeing the work completed as the day draws closer and closer. However, the opposite of this scenario is also true: the woman may be slower, with less fervency, the farther away the wedding day is…and if she is told that the date will be greatly postponed, she may even lose hope, slowing down the work to a stop.

Yet there is something of far greater significance for the Bride of Christ. We have been given the Holy Spirit as a Helper. He is also Jesus' pledge of that divine proposal. Look again at the introductory verse from Revelation. It is not the Bride of Christ *alone* who is saying, "Come." The Holy Spirit in us is actually saying this first. The fervency of the work that needs to be accomplished, which takes place through faith in the soon return of Jesus, *initiates with the Holy Spirit.* The Holy Spirit of God has equal intensity for the salvation and discipleship of the lost as Jesus did when He walked on earth. The Holy Spirit in us is not longing to leave this evil place merely to be gone from here. *He longs for the lost.*

The Spirit and the Bride Say "Come"...to Whom?

Any intense desire in our hearts for those who have yet to believe in Jesus first comes from and was birthed in us by the Holy Spirit. He longs to bear witness to the multitudes of the work of Jesus through the Gospel. Thus, as we join with the Holy Spirit in saying, *"Come quickly, Lord Jesus"* (see Revelation 22:20), we will be participating in the anointing of the Holy Spirit, our Helper, to take in the harvest of nations. For the Gospel message of justice and mercy possesses also the message of a wedding, which will cause a longing within the lost who hear to also say, *"Come."* And they themselves will long to come to that wedding …

> *"The kingdom of heaven may be compared to a king, who gave a wedding feast for his son. And he sent out his slaves to call those who had been invited to the wedding feast, and they were unwilling to come. Again he sent out other slaves saying, 'Tell those who have been invited, "Behold, I have prepared my dinner; my oxen and my fattened livestock are all butchered and everything is ready; come to the wedding feast." ' But they paid no attention and went their way, one to his own farm, another to his business, and the rest seized his slaves and mistreated them and killed them. But the king was enraged and sent his armies, and destroyed those murderers, and set their city on fire. Then he said to his slaves, 'The wedding is ready, but those who were invited were not worthy. Go therefore to the main highways, and as many as you find there, invite to the wedding feast.' And those slaves went out into, the streets and gathered together all they*

Promised Joy, Promised Judgment

found, both evil and good; and the wedding hall was filled with dinner guests."

Matthew 22:2-10

As in the story of Esther, when the Bride realizes that she needs her Husband to get the work of justice done, and that she cannot do it apart from Him, she will passionately long to see Him. And when He finally comes to her and renders that final judgment against the Haman of this earth, then the Groom, who is King of kings, will sit together with His Bride. Ultimate justice will have been rendered to introduce the age to come. Not only will the Bride have rightly longed for her Love, she will have brought alongside those who heard the Gospel message for the first time when they were invited to a wedding feast…those who were thirsty, those who had no money, those who were weary.

Indeed, those who never before had an audience with such royalty will find themselves at the wedding.

Twelve

One Man, One Thousand Demons and One City...Meet Jesus

"But if I cast out demons by the finger of God, then the kingdom of God has come upon you."
Luke 11:20

The Son of God appeared for this purpose, that He might destroy the works of the devil.
1 John 3:8b

The justice of God, as it is carried out, is violent. The examples of the Old Testament accounts, such as Moses against Egypt, Joshua against the Canaanites, and David against the Philistines, are lessons to the Church today of spiritual battles against the kingdom of darkness. The weapons of our current warfare, however, are not as in the days of old; for we are not fighting against man, but against principalities and powers in the heavenly places (see Ephesians 6:12).

Nevertheless, these present day battles must be

fought with the weapons of God. The mindset, then, for this kind of warfare is entirely different from the physical, natural-world situations we seem to more easily understand. To defeat the kingdom of darkness, those people under the rule of King Jesus must dispossess the enemy and then repossess the very areas once held under Satan's rule. However, this kind of wording may bring one into wrong concepts of the spiritual fight if our purpose for Kingdom warfare is misunderstood.

We do not fight to the point where we leave people wounded and killed, emotionally and spiritually, as in natural warfare. We are fighting to literally see lives transformed from hopelessness to hope and faith and life when the victory is gained. Again, even these words alone can be construed to connote only a spiritual rebirth, leaving the physical realities of this life untouched. Do not misunderstand me. I do not negate whatsoever the truth of spiritual rebirth. But I am addressing the perspective that only sees mindsets changed without seeing "real world" issues changed.

When the preaching of the Gospel is limited to mere lessons in morals and ethics, then the impact of God's justice on earth will also be limited. I know this bothers some people. Nevertheless, there are presently many regions of this earth where moral Gospel preaching alone is not effective enough. Then is the Gospel weaker than the reality of the kingdom of darkness? Not at all!

The powerlessness does not lie with the Gospel, but with those who believe in the limited ability of the message in this modern day, as opposed to the message as it was preached with signs and wonders during the lives of Jesus and the apostles.

Cities all over the earth are in desperate need of a

mighty move of the Holy Spirit in which the reality of the force of God's justice becomes evident to all. When this happens, though, there will assuredly arise some "religious" people who will attribute the power of God to the devil, even as some did in Jesus' day (see Matthew 12:24). However, God will have won the hearts of those who are desperate for His justice. They are the ones He seeks anyway (Mark 2:17).

The transformation of cities in the New Testament is evidenced by the *demonstration* of God's justice through the power of God initially working to set one or a few individuals free from the clutches of Satan. These testimonies are seen in the life of Jesus in the gospels. Notice the impact of the power of God on the city.

> *And they sailed to the country of the Gerasenes, which is opposite Galilee. And when He had come out onto the land, He was met by a certain man from the city who was possessed with demons; and who had not put on any clothing for a long time, and was not living in a house, but in the tombs.*
>
> *And seeing Jesus, he cried out and fell before Him, and said in a loud voice, "What do I have to do with You, Jesus, Son of the Most High God? I beg You, do not torment me." For He had been commanding the unclean spirit to come out of the man. For it had seized him many times; and he was bound with chains and shackles and kept under guard; and yet he would burst his fetters and be driven by the demon into the desert.*
>
> *And Jesus asked him, "What is your name?"*

Promised Joy, Promised Judgment

And he said, "Legion"; for many demons had entered him. And they were entreating Him not to command them to go depart into the abyss.

Now there was a herd of many swine feeding there on the mountain; and the demons entreated Him to permit them to enter the swine. And He gave them permission. And the demons came out from the man and entered the swine; and the herd rushed down the steep bank into the lake, and were drowned. Luke 8:26-33

This is the only time in the entire New Testament that it is recorded that Jesus went into Decapolis, an area east of the Jordan located southeast of the Sea of Galilee. But this one work of God's justice dispossessed the kingdom of darkness, which was not only raging within this man, but was ruling the entire area with fear and terror.

And when the herdsmen saw what had happened, they ran away and reported it in the city and out in the country. And the people went out to see what had happened; and they came to Jesus, and found the man from whom the demons had gone out, sitting down at the feet of Jesus, clothed and in his right mind; and they became frightened. And those who had seen it reported to them how the man who was demon-possessed had been made well. And all the people of the country of the Gerasenes and the surrounding district asked Him to depart from them; for they were gripped with great fear; and He got into a boat, and returned. But the man from whom the

demons had gone out was begging Him that he might accompany Him; but He sent him away, saying, "Return to your house and describe what great things God has done for you." And he went away, proclaiming throughout the whole city what great things Jesus had done for him.
Luke 8:34-39

Mark finishes the account this way:

And he went away and began to proclaim in Decapolis what great things Jesus had done for him; AND EVERYONE MARVELED.
Mark 5:20

When that one man was repossessed for the Kingdom of God, it was enough to change the cities on that side of the Jordan. You see, the Decapolis was not just one city. By the name's very definition, it was ten cities.

When Jesus had brought the violent working of God's justice to bear to set this one man free, the whole region's population was shaken. In fact, they were so shaken by this greater authority than that which had raged in the demon-possessed man that they could not even hear the message of the Gospel through the Man of God who had come to bring them joy. And Jesus knew this. But He still didn't give the ground He had taken back to the enemy.

The power of God had changed one man's life. The principalities in the heavens over that region were confronted and booted out. Jesus told the man, who had first-hand experience of this greater Kingdom authority, to go back to his home and proclaim the power of

Promised Joy, Promised Judgment

God's Kingdom. What was his home? It was his city!

> *"RETURN TO YOUR HOUSE and describe what great things God has done for you." And he went away, proclaiming throughout the whole city what great things Jesus had done for him.*
>
> Luke 8:39

The city met Jesus, the Son of God…and the authority of His Kingdom with the evidenced power of God.

Beloved, if Jesus needed this kind of miraculous authority to back up His words, how much more do we need it? The same demons that needed to "feel" the justice of God in Jesus' day are still around. And they are not easily moved out of an area. They must be violently kicked out. This kind of action does not come with charisma of personality, but by the mighty working of God's Holy Spirit in us.

We must understand the true heavenly nature of justice and judgment, as well as the true nature of Satan and his demons, if we are to understand that a "moral" Gospel alone does not make for Kingdom replacement. Evil, wicked, immoral, violent leaders are not moved out by words of compromise. The natural world bears witness to that fact. Strong men who lead by wickedness only understand strength, not mere words. Satan is by far a more vicious and conniving leader than any human being has been. He only bears witness to a stronger Leader *by the force* of that stronger Leader.

> *When a strong man, fully armed, guards his own homestead, his possessions are undisturbed; BUT when someone stronger than he attacks him and*

overpowers him, he takes away from him all his armor on which he had relied, and distributes his plunder. He who is not with Me is against Me; and he who does not gather with Me, scatters.
Luke 11:21-23

We would all agree that Jesus is the stronger "Someone." But what is the context of this verse? It concerns *God's present, flowing, demonstrative power.* If Jesus were speaking of Kingdom replacement through the working of His power, and in the same breath declaring that all who are not with Him in this are against Him and are thus scatterers, then where does this leave the doctrine of Jesus' power not being for today? The gatherers are those who join with Him in His power to overcome the devil and take his plunder.

Do you want a harvest to gather in? Are you, then, a gatherer or a scatterer? That is, where do you stand on the power of God today to accomplish the work of gathering, as the above story from Luke describes? You must absolutely consider the *lifestyle* example of Jesus in winning the cities of Decapolis. If words alone, without the demonstration of God's power, were not sufficient for Jesus in His day, a day when city populations were a fraction of what they are in today's megalopolises, then how are we today going to win our cities with only a moral Gospel which possesses no demonstrative power from Heaven to back up Heaven's words? It is entirely not the nature of such a supernatural God to think this way. Why would a God who has moved with such tremendous power since the day this creation first existed decide to halt *His* power because of *our* so-called greater modern-day understanding? Those who know the active power of the kingdom of darkness in regions of the world where it is an everyday occurrence stand back and mock. *Justice without the power to back it up is not Kingdom of God justice!*

God desires to validate His Word with *His* demonstration of the power of His Word. It is not His will for us to attempt to accomplish His work alone (see Mark 16:20).

> *"When the Helper comes, whom I will send to you from the Father, that is the Spirit of truth, who proceeds from the Father, He will bear witness of Me…"* John 15:26

Jesus promised us a Helper—to bear witness in and through us of *Him*. How does this indwelling Holy Spirit, our Helper from Heaven, bear witness of Jesus?

> *God also bearing witness with them, both by signs and wonders and BY VARIOUS MIRACLES AND BY GIFTS OF THE HOLY SPIRIT according to His own will.* Hebrews 2:4

Beloved, it is time once again today for peoples, cities and demons…to meet Jesus!

Thirteen

The Judge, the Accused and the Judging Accusers

Without question, we would all agree that God in Heaven is the ultimate Judge of man. Although the Scripture speaks much about judgments, both those in history and those to come, it is also without question that this Judge in Heaven is One who is ever willing to extend His hand of mercy to any guilty party who would reach out for it (see Hebrews 4:16). The throne room, as we have seen, is a place where judgment is meted out. But it is equally a place where mercy is poured out. He who sits on the throne is not first a Judge, but a Creator and Father to man. And so it is that He would have us be like Him…not judges, but mercy-givers. The heart of God in this matter was expressed through the words of Jesus:

> *"Blessed are the merciful, for they shall receive mercy."* Matthew 5:7

Promised Joy, Promised Judgment

Any of us would desire mercy to be extended to us whenever we are found guilty of sin. But sometimes it is difficult to extend our hands in mercy to those we view as blatant sinners—especially when we have lived a generally clean and moral life, and thus hold ourselves to be the standard of righteousness by which others ought to live. Those who have lived a religious life can easily find themselves judging by that standard, without regard for those who know little or nothing of religion. The standard by which we view our fellow man, our fellow sin-*full* man, cannot be our own religious walk of never having really "sinned" like those around us. For then we become, not a righteous judge, as God is a Judge, but an accuser, a finger-pointer. Prayers for the lost, if they even come out of our mouths, are probably not tempered with mercy. Indeed, we can even find ourselves pointing the finger at fellow believers for not living up to our standard.

> *For we are not bold to class or compare ourselves with some of those who commend themselves; but when they measure themselves by themselves, and compare themselves with themselves, they are without understanding.*
> 2 Corinthians 10:12

Paul contends that if we place ourselves as the standard by which we measure others, then we are without understanding. Please do not misunderstand me. It is not that we must always feel as though we are under condemnation, in hopes of walking humbly before God and men. It is rather that we must not make our own goodness the measure for every person who passes by.

Such measure will be the standard set against us by God. He will hold *us* to *our* standard when we judge another (or really, accuse another) according to the measure of our own good.

The deception of our seeming knowledge of good and evil when we judge according to ourselves is that this standard stems from the tree of the knowledge of good and evil. Do you remember who ate from that tree? That tree did not consist of the knowledge of evil alone, but of both good *and* evil. And it certainly did not give life to the eater! If we judge by the standard of good and evil, we minister death and not life to the person we judge. Furthermore, we will be judged by that same standard. If the Law becomes the standard that we require everyone to live up to, God will require of us that we fulfill every jot and tittle of that very Law. The warning by Jesus is clear:

"Do not judge lest you be judged. For in the way you judge, you will be judged; AND BY YOUR STANDARD OF MEASURE, IT WILL BE MEASURED TO YOU." Matthew 7:1-2

The opposite also is true:

"Be merciful, just as your Father is merciful. And do not judge and you will not be judged; and do not condemn, and you will not be condemned; pardon, and you will be pardoned. Give, and it will be given to you; good measure, pressed down, shaken together, running over, they will pour into your lap. For by your standard of measure it will be measured to you in return." Luke 6:36-38

Promised Joy, Promised Judgment

If your standard of measure is full of mercy to pour out upon your fellow man, you will find the same being poured out to you.

Is the implication here, then, that we should ignore sin around us in our society for the sake of showing mercy to everyone? To the contrary. We must cry out for God's standard, His character, which is righteousness, justice, equity and, with these, mercy. Jesus always called sin exactly what it was. For those who would turn from it, forgiveness of sin poured out from Him to set them free from sin's power, so that they should not walk again in that place of bondage. But Jesus also confronted the attitude within those who held their own religiosity as the godly standard by which men should lead their lives, because that attitude contained nothing within that could show mercy to set the sinner free, but only condemnation with a mind for judgment.

There is an account in the gospel of John that demonstrates this attitude of those who make themselves the standard—the judge and the accuser—and by it become the accused.

Jesus had gone into the Temple one morning to teach the people when the scribes and Pharisees burst in on the scene, dragging along a disgraced and embarrassed woman. Though they planned to make a spectacle of her, it was not primarily her they wanted to condemn in accusing judgment. This religious group of men had already pronounced judgment upon her in their minds. They wanted to discredit the seemingly overly merciful Jesus in the eyes of the crowds. They would throw the very Law of Moses right into the face of Jesus in hopes of getting Him to inadvertently denounce it, thereby proving that He was against Moses, a man whom God had anointed and to whom God had given the Law.

The scribes and Pharisees interrupted Jesus' teaching, pushing the woman forward for all to see. Follow what happens next…

> …*they said to Him, "Teacher, this woman has been caught in adultery, in the very act. Now in the Law Moses commanded us to stone such women; what then do You say?" And they were saying this, testing Him, in order that they might have grounds for accusing Him. But Jesus stooped down, and with His finger wrote on the ground.*
>
> *But when they persisted in asking Him, He straightened up, and said to them, "He who is without sin among you, let him be the first to throw a stone at her."*
>
> *Again He stooped down, and wrote on the ground. And when they heard it, they began to go out one by one, beginning with the older ones, and He was left alone, and the woman, where she had been, in the midst.*
>
> *And straightening up, Jesus said to her, "Woman, where are they? Did no one condemn you?"*
>
> *And she said, "No one, Lord."*
>
> *And Jesus said, "Neither do I condemn you; go your way. From now on sin no more."*
>
> John 8:4-11

When we dare to set ourselves up as the standard by which we judge others, we have placed ourselves on the judgment seat as an accusing judge. We care only about sentencing the accused to our condemnation. There is no honest desire for mercy in this kind of earthly judgment. If there had been any desire to pardon, the standard of self-righteousness would never have been set up in the first place. Thus it was that Jesus held these men to their own standard, and they clearly heard the judgment against their own hearts. For the same God who said in the Law of Moses, *"You shall not commit adultery"* (Exodus 20:14), also said, through Jesus, that *"everyone who looks on a woman to lust for her has committed adultery with her already in his heart"* (Matthew 5:28).

The oldest among the woman's accusers were the first to leave, for their levels of guilt, according to the standard of the Law to which they held the woman, were higher. They knew they themselves were guilty with those last words from Jesus' lips. These accusers grudgingly realized that their accusing hand pointing the finger at the woman also had three fingers pointing back at themselves.

Jesus did not say that this woman was innocent. But He first dealt with those who had placed themselves in the position of being her judge, allowing them to be judged first by that Law, written in stone, that they held so dearly.

Jesus is the true Judge (see John 5:22). His judgments will either set us free or publicly hold us guilty for our judgment of others. Our judgments of one another, the very words that come out of our mouths, must therefore be based on the standard by which we desire His judgment upon us. Our prayers must be tempered by this Judge's standard, which stems from the desire for justice *and* mercy, a desire based on the tree of life, not the tree of the knowledge of good and evil. This is no blind eye which does not see sin for what it is, but it carries a heart that desires truth in the inward parts of our fellowman. Some will reject the goodness of God extended through us. And we can see that for what it is. The issue here is false accusation, a judgment based on the standard of false religiosity which causes the accusing judge to be self-exalted for his own goodness in comparison to the one being judged.

Some of Jesus' harshest words as recorded in the gospels were reserved for those among the religious community. This was not because He disliked them or their religion. Rather, He was exposing the false religion of their walk before God, their facade of the "appearances of religion" in the eyes of men instead of truth in the inward parts, where God sees.

> *"Woe to you, scribes and Pharisees, hypocrites! For you tithe mint and dill and cummin, and have neglected the weightier provisions of the law: justice and mercy and faithfulness; but these are the things you should have done without neglecting the others."* Matthew 23:23

The Pharisees and scribes boasted of the way in which they kept the Law—especially where it concerned the appearances before men. Jesus told them, however, that if they were going to keep the Law, they were to keep all of it. That included what He called the *"weightier provisions"* of the Law, which are justice *and* mercy *and* faithfulness. These are things not so apparent to the eyes of men, yet which speak the loudest to God, the Judge of all.

It is easy to boast of ourselves when we "do" all the right things; but we may be doing them only to be noticed by men. Those are the times it is easiest to criticize others who do not measure up. Jesus was not telling the Pharisees to neglect the things they had been doing; but in the midst of those things, they were not to forget about justice, mercy and faithfulness, all of which have to do with the character of the heart. Jesus' judgment is not based on the standard of the tree of the knowledge of good and evil, although He may allow us to be judged by that standard if we hold others to it. But this is not His standard, for its end result is always death. Christ's standard comes from the tree of life, a judgment that offers *life* to all people! Everyone must come to the Judge to receive justice and mercy according to His standard…and by it we will be changed so that we also bring forth from the tree of life.

The judging accuser still waits, as the serpent in the garden, hanging from that other tree; he always waits for us to trap others in a judgment of condemnation. If we want to be judged by Jesus so as not to be condemned, we must hold out to others a standard of justice by which we do not condemn them. In other words, if we want to eat of the tree of life, we must also give the fruit of that tree to our fellowman (see Galatians 5:22-23). The folly of those who walk as accusing judges, who leave no place for mercy in their ridicule of others, eventually becomes evident. God is not mocked by such false religiosity. He will allow this foolishness to rise to the surface to be judged by Him. He will cause it to be exposed for what it is in the eyes of even the ones who bore the brunt of those false religious standards.

And as He passed by, He saw a man blind from birth. And His disciples asked Him, saying,

> *"Rabbi, who sinned, this man or his parents, that he should be born blind?"* John 9:1-2

Jesus replied to His disciples that no one had sinned in this case. He then went on to heal the man; only it was on a Sabbath day, which, as far as the Pharisees were concerned, was the same as working on a day when no one was supposed to work. They summoned the healed man into their council chambers in order to obtain some kind of evidence to judge Jesus for "breaking the Law."

> *So a second time they called the man who had been blind, and said to him, "Give glory to God; we know that this man is a sinner."*
> *He therefore answered, "Whether He is a sinner, I do not know; one thing I do know, that whereas I was blind, now I see."*
> *They said therefore to him, "What did He do to you? How did He open your eyes?"*
> *He answered them, "I told you already, and you did not listen; why do you want to hear it again? You do not want to become His disciples too, do you?"*
> *And they reviled him, and said, "You are his disciple, but we are the disciples of Moses. We know that God has spoken to Moses; but as for this man, we do not know where He is from."*
> John 9:24-29

The Pharisees concluded that this healed man was just as deluded and as much a sinner as they had judged Jesus to be. They kicked him out of their chambers. Jesus found him again as he wandered around in the Temple, enjoying seeing this building for the first time in his life. Jesus spoke to the man about Himself. The man believed in Him, humbling his heart in reverential worship of God. It was here that Jesus called the folly of the Pharisees for what it was, showing *them* to be truly under judgment.

> *And Jesus said, "For judgment I came into this world, that those who do not see may see; and that those who see may become blind."*
>
> *Those of the Pharisees who were with Him heard these things, and said to Him, "We are not blind too, are we?"*
>
> *Jesus said to them, "If you were blind, you would have no sin; but since you say, 'We see,' your sin remains."*   John 9:39-41

The religious zealots of Jesus' time were so adamant about holding the common people to the letter of the Law of Moses that they did not care what kindness was shown on any Sabbath day, even if that kindness meant saving a life. (See also Luke 13:10-17.) But Jesus' healing of this blind man was itself a judgment against them. They desired the letter of the Law, which only bears the fruit of condemnation, rather than the tree of life, which ministers life and healing and freedom from the bondages of religious shackles and the shackles of sin.

The false religion of self-righteousness which condemns those who do not look like us will cause us to become enemies of those who are set free by Jesus. Eventually we may even find ourselves to be the enemies of Christ Himself. In a short time, those accusing judges of Jesus' day would violently use their positions against Him. The result, as they intended, would be a judgment of condemnation, a sentence of death. This bore witness to the fact that they were judges born from the serpent who longs for just such a sentence upon mankind.

But the sentence of condemnation upon *this* Man would produce an unintended result for all mankind. This Man would bear for mankind the fullness of the devil's condemnation, the false judgment of judging accusers, *and* the true judgment for sin which had been upon man since the garden. The result for all who believe would be the fruit of the tree of life—from which God has always intended for man to eat.

Fourteen

The Seed of the Woman: Fulfilling the First Judgment

"Now judgment is upon this world; now the ruler of this world shall be cast out. And I, if I be lifted up from the earth, will draw all men to Myself."
John 12:31-32

The thing Adam and his wife needed which would benefit them was judgment, although initially it would not appear so. Judgment was the very action that would free them from their bondage to the sin they had submitted to. That first couple died as a result of that first disobedient decision against God's command ... and so all their children and their descendents would die because they too were under the penalty for sin. But the Creator had made a promise to the couple, through His judgment of the serpent, that one day a Child would be born who would bring eternal hope back to man. Yet the serpent would render a blow against that Man-child who would attempt to break his power.

Promised Joy, Promised Judgment

"And I will put enmity between you and the woman, and between your seed and her seed; he shall bruise you on the head, and you shall bruise him on the heel." Genesis 3:15

Generation after generation passed. Many prophets, prophetic words and prophetic acts continually came to the cities with the promise of a Man who would one day come to finally fulfill the first judgment spoken so long before. The free rule of the serpent to do his works seemed to go unchecked throughout the history of man...except in the lives of a people called the Hebrews, and some few others who came into direct contact with them.

But the promised fulfillment of that first judgment was growing in very specific ways. God in Heaven was single-minded and unmoved from His word to bruise the serpent's head through the Seed of a woman. He was letting the generations know that eternal hope was not a never-to-be reality. God was adamantly showing that the words and works of power the Hebrews experienced throughout their history were prophetic signs of His judgment against the serpent. One day the serpent's stranglehold on man would come under manifested judgment and be broken once and for all. This promised act fulfilled would prove that all divine justice for man, manifested through the preaching of the Gospel down to this very day, would have a basis of authority.

In one particular Old Testament account the prophetic judgment is clear. The sons of Israel were coming out of Egypt when rebellion broke out. They came against Moses, asking why he had brought them out of

Egypt if the alternative was to starve or die of thirst in the wilderness. This was during the time when God was providing manna for them daily!

Needless to say, God was not pleased with this attitude.

> *And the LORD sent fiery serpents among the people and they bit the people, so that many people of Israel died. So the people came to Moses and said, "We have sinned, because we have spoken against the LORD and you; intercede with the LORD, that He may remove the serpents from us." And Moses interceded for the people.*
>
> *Then the LORD said to Moses, "Make a fiery serpent, and set it on a standard; and it shall come about, that everyone who is bitten, when he looks at it, he shall live." And Moses made a bronze serpent and set it on the standard; and it came about, that if a serpent bit any man, when he looked to the bronze serpent, he lived.*
>
> Numbers 21:6-9

The similarity between this Old Testament occurrence and the cross of Christ is obvious.

> *"And as Moses lifted up the serpent in the wilderness, even so must the Son of Man be lifted up; so that whoever believes may in Him have ETERNAL LIFE.* John 3:14-15

But that prophetic sign of Moses' day was not understood by either the people or the demons on the day it was fulfilled, for they didn't know that the Seed of the woman was walking among them.

The hour of the judgment of Genesis 3:15 was at hand. It was the hour in the age of this earth in which the most defined justice, the most violent judgment, the most pronounced victory, would be decided once for all eternity. The hour of *THE* judgment needed by man and required by God had finally come to the earth. The Seed of the woman was now in flesh and blood, present among men. The time was fulfilled for Him to face, as the first Adam had, the enemy of men's souls. This Man would have to overcome the enemy *in flesh and blood*, or there could never again be any eternal hope for anyone.

But to whom did the hour of judgment belong? Listen to the words of the Seed of the woman who was chosen to carry out God's ultimate judgment against the serpent:

> *"Now My soul has become troubled; and what shall I say, 'Father, save Me from this hour'? BUT FOR THIS PURPOSE I CAME TO THIS HOUR."*
> John 12:27

> *And Jesus said to the chief priests and officers of the temple and elders who had come against Him, "Have you come out with swords and clubs as you would against a robber? While I was with you daily in the temple, you did not lay hands on Me; BUT THIS HOUR AND THE POWER OF DARKNESS ARE YOURS."* Luke 22:52-53

The hour of judgment for which Jesus had come was an hour of the power of darkness. This was a place not

THE SEED OF THE WOMAN: FULFILLING THE FIRST JUDGMENT

on Jesus' turf, as it were, but clearly on the devil's turf. To the natural eye, Jesus was to fight a battle, render judgment and win—but in an arena in which it seemed absolutely impossible to gain a victory. When it came right down to it, it would even seem that in the end He lost....

But this battle was not one to be watched by the natural eye. The Seed of the woman would fulfill the first judgment against the serpent without so much as lifting a breath to the serpent. God's justice would come forth for man in a way that would perplex both man and serpent. For herein is the irony of this "first judgment" fulfillment: *The Seed of the woman would bear the penalty of that first judgment FOR man* to bring about both God's kind of justice for man and God's first judgment against the serpent. You see, the justice of God that needed to be satisfied was not a direct battle against Satan, though Satan would be intimately involved in the battle. The paradox was that the battle which the serpent was ready to fight would not even look to the serpent like a fight at all, but merely a surrender to him.

There was one issue, however, that had to be taken care of before the justice of God could be fulfilled through Christ in such a battle. The power of Satan over man was death—because of sin. Every man but One who was ever born up to this point in history had sinned, thus disqualifying them from even entering the ring.

> *...for all have sinned and fall short of the glory of God...*   Romans 3:23

The problem is that everyone who has ever been

born of the seed of Adam has sinned. No one who has had Adam as a father could ever be worthy enough to satisfy God's justice. It was God's demand that the justice needed to be satisfied in order to set man free from sin and give him eternal life could only be accomplished through a man without sin. Only in this case would the serpent have no claim. Only such a sacrifice would be perfect and acceptable.

So how could anyone help...ever?

The clue is found in the words spoken to the serpent.

> *"And I will put enmity between you and the woman, and between your seed and her seed...."*
> Genesis 3:15

It was not that this would be accomplished by one born of the seed of Adam. The promise was to *"her seed."* Adam heard this; thus he prophetically bestowed upon his wife the name *"Eve."* This name, which means, "mother of all the living," bore testimony to this prophetic promise. But a miracle would be needed to somehow accomplish this kind of birth! One would need to be born of woman, apart from man, so as not to have the seed of the sin nature passed on to the child.

We will not look here in much detail at the birth of Jesus. But we do know that Isaiah prophesied that a virgin would bear a Son, whose name would be *"Immanuel,"* or "God with us" (see Isaiah 7:14). This prophecy was fulfilled (see Matthew 1:18-25).

Mary gave birth to a Boy who had none of the seed of Adam. Joseph, Mary's husband, who was of the lineage of Adam, would not intimately know Mary until after this Baby's birth (see Matthew 1:25). (Read Luke

1:26-35 to understand God's working of this miracle.) Still, this Immanuel, this "God with us" human would also have to be wholly a man, or else it could be said that the standard for God's justice to be satisfied would not be just at all. This Immanuel could not be a God of *self-contained* might in the flesh, but had to be a Man *in the likeness of sinful flesh, who would be tempted as any man*...but He would never give in to the temptations of the serpent in any way whatsoever. Jesus was that Immanuel, that "God with us," not by virtue of power, but by virtue of seed, so as not to have sin-contaminated blood. He was thus the *"second Adam,"* and would be tempted, in His perfection, even as the first Adam had been tempted in his perfection (see Matthew 4:1-11).

> *Since then we have a great high priest who has passed through the heavens, JESUS THE SON OF GOD, let us hold fast our confession. For we do not have a high priest who cannot sympathize with our weaknesses, BUT ONE WHO HAS BEEN TEMPTED IN ALL THINGS AS WE ARE, YET WITHOUT SIN.* Hebrews 4:14-15

Jesus walked like us, and was tempted as we have been, yet *He did not sin*!

This Seed of the woman was on the devil's territory—at least, the devil thinks it belongs to him. But He did not fall into the devil's trap as did the first Adam. And this second Adam really was a Man without self-contained divine power.

> *"...Christ Jesus, who, although He existed in the*

form of God, DID NOT REGARD EQUALITY WITH GOD A THING TO BE GRASPED, BUT EMPTIED HIMSELF, taking the form of a bond-servant, and being made in the likeness of men.
                                                                                    Philippians 2:5-7

Since then the children share in flesh and blood, HE HIMSELF LIKEWISE ALSO PARTOOK OF THE SAME, that through death He might render powerless him who had the power of death, that is, the devil.... Therefore, He had to be made like His brethren IN ALL THINGS, that He might become a merciful and faithful high priest in things pertaining to God, to make propitiation for the sins of the people.   Hebrews 2:14, 17

Finally there was a Man, the Seed of the woman spoken of through the ages, made in the likeness of all men, yet without sin.

The hour of judgment was at last upon the earth. Indeed, this very hour was *the hour* for which this Man had come. It was an hour of darkness that belonged to the serpent, but an hour in which even the serpent was in complete darkness. The hour of judgment, a sentence pronounced against the serpent in Eden, was coming to fulfillment. So also being fulfilled was the prophetic act by the Creator so long ago to cover the nakedness of the flesh of sinful man. The shame of the nakedness of sin was about to be displayed before the eyes of mocking men and demons. The *covering* for that shame was about to be displayed, not in the continued need for the pouring out of the blood of animals, but in *ONE* sacrifice for all mankind in the shed blood of this one sinless Man. The serpent had thought he'd won over man for all time in the garden. But that garden of God was a picture of another garden of God where the first drops of blood for the deserved eternal judgment of mankind would be spilled. Both the Garden of Eden and the Garden of Gethsemane were the initiation points for the planned redemption of man...and the planned judgment of the serpent.

> *And they came to a place named Gethsemane [a place on the Mount of Olives meaning "oil-press"]; and He said to His disciples, "Sit here until I have prayed." And He took with Him Peter and James and John, and began to be very distressed and troubled. And He said to them, "My soul is deeply grieved to the point of death; remain here and keep watch." And He went a little beyond them, and fell to the ground, and began to pray that if it were possible, the hour might pass Him by. And He was saying, "Abba! Father! All things are possible for Thee; remove this cup from Me; yet not what I will, but what Thou wilt."*
> Mark 14:32-36

> *Now an angel from heaven appeared to Him, strengthening Him. And being in agony He was praying very fervently; and His sweat became like drops of blood, falling down upon the ground.*
> Luke 22:43-44

Look at Jesus' prayer closely. He spoke the truth: "*Father! All things are possible for Thee.*" All things were indeed possible with God...except this? Was this *the only possible justice that was able to pay for man's sins so that man could gain eternal life and relationship with his Creator?* Look at Matthew's wording of this particular account:

> *And He went a little beyond them, and fell on His face and prayed, saying, "My Father, if it is possible, let this cup pass from Me; yet not as I will, but as Thou wilt."* Matthew 26:39

It was possible, beloved, for Jesus to have let this cup of judgment pass, but that would have meant there could be no redemption for man: thus Jesus' words "*yet not as I will, but as Thou wilt.*" The issue here was the will of God the Father. And His will was to bring about the fulfillment of His promise to man given in the Garden of Eden.

Father God would ache in a way I don't think we'll ever comprehend as He watched His Son become sin for the entirety of mankind. Yet He knew, as a God of justice, that there was *no other possible way* for mankind's sin to be paid for in full, for justice to be satisfied, for mercy to have its foundation. Even if another man were to suffer for eternity to pay for his sin, it would never suffice because the blood of man already possesses in itself the guilt of sin. Therefore it could not be sufficient to satisfy eternal justice. Holy, pure, guilt-free blood was needed to accomplish that eternal task.

Father God was seeking a return to the relationship that had been cut off by the disobedience of man in Eden. Every person born after Adam has had within him a likeness of Creator God. Yet God could not send a person made in His image into an eternal Hell without making a way to redeem that person. To understand this even a little is to begin to comprehend His heartache each time one made in His image rejects Him to choose an eternity apart from Him. This also helps us to see a little of how He could send His Son, made into the image of sinful human flesh, to be nailed to a cross and die a mortal's death. For Almighty God, knowing the beginning of this finite age to its end, knew that after the suffering of death and satisfaction of justice, His Son could *not* be held in an eternal grip of death.

The hour of the power of darkness was filled to the full. Every demon in every place, I am sure, was gathered together to witness what they believed would be their greatest triumph…and God in Heaven would have it no other way. He wanted all of them to behold this spectacle, this judgment poured out upon Jesus. The demons would make sure that a representative from every lawful and lawless, religious and pagan, class of society was present to observe this moment in history. And they would use every available voice from each of these groups of people to make sure their plan, as they thought, was fully realized.

All those gathered watched as Pilate called for the chief priests and the rulers to declare his finding of innocence for Jesus. They heard him offer to release Jesus to the people. And they cheered along with the crowds who called for Barabbas the rebel to be released in His stead.

Even though Pilate could find nothing in Jesus worthy of the sentence of death, he bowed to the will of the people.

> *And Pilate, wanting to release Jesus, addressed them again, but they kept on calling out, saying, "Crucify, crucify Him!"*

Promised Joy, Promised Judgment

> *And he said to them the third time, "Why, what evil has this man done? I have found in Him no guilt demanding death; I will therefore punish Him and release Him."*
>
> *But they were insistent, with loud voices asking that He be crucified. And their voices began to prevail. And Pilate pronounced sentence that their demand be granted.* Luke 23:20-24

So Pilate released the murderer and delivered the innocent Christ to the will of the people.

> *And when they came to the place called The Skull, there they crucified Him and the criminals, one on the right and the other on the left.*
> Luke 23:33

Pilate himself, the chief arbiter of public justice, pronounced with his own mouth that Jesus had no guilt. Although he did eventually pronounce the death sentence against Jesus, *God made sure that everyone, man and demon alike, heard that His Son had no guilt!* Thus, this Man in whom was no blemish of sin was stripped (see Matthew 27:35) to take on the shame of every person's sin, from the first couple back in Eden who knew of their nakedness because of sin to the last person yet to be born. And every vileness of mankind, with all the help that hell could muster, was poured upon this one fully sinless, fully just, Man (see Romans 5:6, 8, 10; 2 Corinthians 5:21).

King David, a thousand years earlier, had prophesied concerning this hour:

My God, my God, why hast Thou forsaken me?

THE SEED OF THE WOMAN: FULFILLING THE FIRST JUDGMENT

Far from my deliverance are the words of my groaning. …I am a worm and not a man, a reproach of men, and despised by the people. All who see me sneer at me; they separate with the lip, they wag the head, saying, "Commit yourself to the LORD; let Him deliver him; let Him rescue him, because He delights in him."

Psalm 22:1, 6-8

See Matthew 27:39-47 to see how accurately this prophetic vision by David was fulfilled. David continued:

Be not far from me, for trouble is near; for there is none to help. …They open wide their mouth at me, as a ravening and a roaring lion. I am poured out like water, and all my bones are out of joint; my heart is like wax; it is melted within me. My strength is dried up like a potsherd, and my tongue cleaves to my jaws; and Thou dost lay me in the dust of death. For dogs have surrounded me; a band of evildoers has encompassed me; they pierced my hands and my feet. I can count all my bones. They look, they stare at me; they divide my garments among them, and for my clothing they cast lots. Psalm 22:11, 13-18

Jesus Christ, the Son of Man and the Seed of the woman, was now being lifted up before the eyes of the world, that He might judge the fiery serpent. He was lifted up as the serpent in the wilderness was lifted by Moses, that He might give life to any and all bitten by the serpent, if only they would look up by faith to this One who bore their judgment.

Promised Joy, Promised Judgment

Neither the people nor the demons knew that the divine purposes of almighty, eternal God were being carried out to the letter. They did not perceive the justice of God so violently taking place before their eyes. This kind of wisdom was not understood by any who had eaten from the tree of the knowledge of good and evil, nor was it comprehended by the one who had pushed man into the state of finite understanding.

> *Yet we do speak wisdom among those who are mature; a wisdom, however, not of this age nor of the rulers of this age, who are passing away; but we speak God's wisdom in a mystery, the hidden wisdom which God predestined before the ages to our glory; THE WISDOM WHICH NONE OF THE RULERS OF THIS AGE HAS UNDERSTOOD; FOR IF THEY HAD UNDERSTOOD IT, THEY WOULD NOT HAVE CRUCIFIED THE LORD OF GLORY....*   1 Corinthians 2:6-8

As Jesus was lifted up, hanging by the nails that pierced Him, He was receiving the judgment deserved by man. The serpent thought he was usurping the authority of Immanuel. Yet all the while, this Seed of the woman was bruising the serpent's head, stripping his authority (see Colossians 2:15). Indeed, the physical show of Jesus' nakedness was actually the work of God to strip away the authority of the serpent who had stripped the first Adam of his God-given authority over the earth. Every created being watching—in Heaven, on earth, under the earth, and even to the ends of this creation—believed the Son of God was losing. No one understood that divine justice was being carried out and fully satisfied. For you see, beloved, Jesus, hanging by nails on that wooden cross, never breathed one breath of His life that day on Golgotha against Satan or against man.

> *...it was our grief he bore, our sorrows that weighed him down. And we thought his troubles were a punishment from God, for his own sins! But he was wounded and bruised for our sins. He was beaten that we might have peace; he was lashed—and we were healed! We—every one of us—have strayed away like sheep! We, who left God's paths to follow our own. Yet God laid on him the guilt and sins of every one of us! He was oppressed and he was afflicted, YET HE NEVER SAID A WORD. He was brought as a lamb to the slaughter; and as a sheep before her shearers is dumb, so HE STOOD SILENT before the ones condemning him. From prison and trial they led him away to his death. But who among the people of that day realized it was their sins that he was dying for—that he was suffering their punishment.* Isaiah 53:4-8, The Book

Jesus Christ Himself took the full force of our deserved judgment. And the just God in Heaven, the Father of this just Man hanging there dying for those haters below, *was pleased with this offering.* Why did it satisfy? Why was it pleasing unto God? It pleased God because this Offering had given Himself *willingly* to satisfy justice.

Promised Joy, Promised Judgment

> *But the L<small>ORD</small> was pleased to crush Him, putting Him to grief; if He would render Himself as a guilt offering, He will see His offspring, He will prolong His days, and the good pleasure of the L<small>ORD</small> will prosper in His hand. As a result of the anguish of His soul, He will see it and be satisfied; by His knowledge the Righteous One, My Servant, will justify the many, as He will bear their iniquities. Therefore, I will allot Him a portion with the great, and He will divide the booty with the strong; because He poured out Himself to death, and was numbered with the transgressors; yet He Himself bore the sin of many, and interceded for the transgressors.*   Isaiah 53:10-12

The whole time Jesus was dying on the cross, He was taking the sin of man into His body (Romans 8:3; Hebrews 10:10; 1 Peter 2:24). He was thus rendering mercy for man while accomplishing something incredibly disturbing for the serpent. For when Jesus was hanging on the cross, He was disarming Satan. Satan's power over man, since the Garden of Eden, had been sin—and now this weapon was being stripped right out of his hand. It would take three full days before the old serpent would fully understand this: The accomplishment of sin is death; and Jesus would deal with that on the first day of the week.

> *...having canceled out the certificate of debt consisting of decrees against us and which was hostile to us; and He has taken it out of the way, having nailed it to the cross. When He had disarmed*

the rulers and authorities, HE MADE A PUBLIC DISPLAY OF THEM, having triumphed over them through Him. Colossians 2:14-15

The serpent and his minions thought they were making a public display of the Son of God. But it was Jesus who was making a public display of them! It was at the cross that the serpent lost his hold on man (see Romans 5; 1 Corinthians 15:56-57; Hebrews 9:26). Since that time, it has been the message of the cross that Satan has fought the hardest, for he hates to be reminded of his downfall and his judgment.

Jesus, even as He was on the cross, knew when the justice demanded by the heavenly Judge had been satisfied to the full. From that time on, man would have access to his Creator, an access that had been lost at the beginning of time.

After this, Jesus, knowing that all things had already been accomplished, in order that the Scripture might be fulfilled, said, "I am thirsty." A jar full of sour wine was standing there; so they put a sponge full of the sour wine upon a branch of hyssop, and brought it up to His mouth. When Jesus therefore had received the sour wine, He said, "It is finished!" John 19:28-30a

The full judgment for sin was completed. Jesus looked up once more to His Father.

And Jesus, crying out with a loud voice, said, "Father, INTO THY HANDS I COMMIT MY SPIRIT." And hav-

Promised Joy, Promised Judgment

> *ing said this, He breathed His last. ...And the veil of the temple was torn in two from top to bottom.*   Luke 23:46, Mark 15:38

Beloved, it was for this hour that Jesus came into the world. All of time in this age centers around this one event. And all of eternity will bear the marks, in our Redeemer, of this one single event.

Until then, it is time to let all of mankind know that they must lift their eyes to the cross, where the Seed of the woman broke the power of the serpent from man.

Fifteen

Justice From the Throne: The Role of the Holy Spirit

"When the Helper comes, whom I will send to you from the Father, that is the Spirit of truth, who proceeds from the Father, He will bear witness of Me.... I will send Him to you. And He, when He comes, will convict the world concerning sin, and righteousness and judgment...."

John 15:26; 16:7-8

Jesus declared and demonstrated the justice of the Kingdom of God during His three years of earthly ministry. Although this may not be clearly seen as justice, nevertheless, every teaching and every work of power was God's justice going forth, because Jesus was undoing the works and ramifications of Satan's injustice to man as He ministered to the people (see 1 John 3:8b).

However, there was one crucial event in His life, a supernatural turning point. Before He reached that point, Jesus never performed one single act to show forth Kingdom of God justice. Jesus Himself was literally unable to walk in one iota of Kingdom authority and power until this one supernatural occurrence had taken place. Why was this event so critical? Through it Jesus was letting everyone know that He was fully human. He was demonstrating that He had no self-contained power from Heaven, and that His dependency for His forthcoming service to people was totally upon His Father in Heaven. Further, He was setting an example for *everyone* who would believe in Him afterward. He wanted them to know that they too would have to depend on the Father for the authority and power to spread the message of the Gospel.

This is vitally important, beloved. If you understand *the nature* of Kingdom of God justice, then you will know why this supernatural requirement is also needed in your life. If you walk away saying, "I don't need this," then you will have confessed that you do not understand the true nature of divine justice.

We already know that Jesus walked on earth a sinless Man (see Hebrews 4:15). No true believer can deny this fact. Jesus walked in the character of His heavenly Father. Yet before He began His active ministry of divine service to Israel, Jesus was completely devoid of all supernatural power (see Philippians 2:5-7). Not one miracle or teaching came forth from Him prior to His public ministry. Now, we could still recognize the character of God in Jesus prior to this occurrence. But as incredibly perfect as His lifestyle was, Jesus was not yet capable of bringing change in a way that would *establish and enforce* Kingdom of God justice.

Does this statement sound almost blasphemous? I know some will be shocked at such a remark. But consider this: If Jesus, in His emptied state—in the complete likeness of man, but without the likeness of God in power or authority—was able to bring a change into people's lives, then He would be no different from any "good" man or woman of any era who has sought to bring about social healing. His ministry would thus be a work of the flesh, and not a work of the Spirit of God. It would be a work without eternal consequences for mankind in His time, let alone in any other time. Beyond this, the work of God Himself to reconcile and reestablish relationship with man would never have been accomplished. You see, God's mission was not primarily to make man "good." His mission was to give man eternal life, which is to *"know* [Him], *and Jesus Christ whom* [He had] *sent"* (John 17:3).

There have always been "good" people in every era who have advocated and established ideas to "better" the population. This is not the goal of the Gospel of Jesus Christ. The goal of the Gospel is to proclaim salvation through Christ alone. We are to make all men know that Christ Jesus suffered and died on a cross for mankind's sins; that because of that cross, forgiveness can be proclaimed to all; that whoever chooses to believe and receive the mercy provided by God can now have restored relationship back to the Creator and Redeemer of all mankind. Establishing this truth in men's hearts requires ability beyond man's strength and quality of character. Something beyond mere human strength or words is needed to change the nature of man and to reestablish right relationship with God. Man's "charisma" is not sufficient to accomplish even one small part of this need. If we do not see this, we will so easily fall into the trap of trying to fulfill the requirements of the commission of God to get the Gospel to the nations in our own strength, and we will accomplish very little. We will also be in danger of watering down the Gospel message in order to see greater results.

So are we to simply rely on God and not worry about the development of our character in Christ? No! Rather, this speaks to the issue of establishing the work of the Spirit of God as just that—*the work of the Spirit of God.*

Beloved, no matter what your denominational background may be, you must seriously consider the Church in the book of Acts and ask why they were able to accomplish so much in establishing the Kingdom of God in so many varied places in such a hostile era. And then you must ask the question, Why does it seem that today's Church, in comparison, is accomplishing so much less? Has the Gospel lost its power or effectiveness? Or are we lacking in something that Heaven provided to succeed in this work?

Again, consider honestly the character of Jesus, as godly as He was on earth, and His inaction until a strategic time when something of Heaven was deposited into Him. If the Son of God, perfect as He was as a Man, still needed something of Heaven in order to see mankind restored in relationship to God and to enforce the justice of God on earth against the adversary of men's souls, then how much more do we need the same divine deposit?

What was that crucial supernatural occurrence that happened to Jesus, empowering Him for service?

> *And it came about in those days that Jesus came from Nazareth in Galilee, and was baptized by John in the Jordan. And immediately coming up*

out of the water, He saw the heavens opening, and the Spirit like a dove descending upon Him...
Mark 1:9-10

Jesus was filled with the Holy Spirit of God. He was dependent on the Holy Spirit within to carry out the work of the Gospel, which was the proclamation and demonstration of God's Kingdom. Listen carefully, beloved. You must consider *everything* that Jesus said AND DID in establishing and enforcing the justice of God on earth. We cannot choose only His teachings. His teachings were indeed powerful, yet they were backed up by signs and wonders and miracles! The teachings and the works of power were completely intertwined. Kingdom of God justice was not established through the choosing of one over the other. The very nature of God Himself was exactly represented in Jesus' life and service through His teaching and works of power (see Hebrews 1:3). If Jesus had either fully taught or fully demonstrated the Kingdom signs and wonders alone, He would not have *exactly* represented Father God! Both the teaching and the power gifts were so interwoven in Jesus' ministry that they were often virtually indistinguishable.

> *And they went into Capernaum; and immediately on the Sabbath He entered the synagogue and began to teach. And they were amazed at His teaching; for He was teaching them as one having authority, and not as the scribes.*
> *And just then there was in their synagogue a man with an unclean spirit; and he cried out, saying, "What do we have to do with You, Jesus*

of Nazareth? Have You come to destroy us? I know who You are—the Holy One of God!"

And Jesus rebuked him, saying, "Be quiet, and come out of him!" And throwing him into convulsions, the unclean spirit cried out with a loud voice and came out of him.

And they were all amazed, so that they debated among themselves, saying, "What is this? A NEW TEACHING WITH AUTHORITY! HE COMMANDS EVEN THE UNCLEAN SPIRITS, AND THEY OBEY HIM." Mark 1:21-27

This "*teaching with authority*" included a work of power to cast out a demon. The people were amazed at this teaching, which was intertwined with the demonstration of God's justice. Many years later, Paul the apostle copied this pattern to entwine teaching and power, showing the true character of Father God.

…they found a certain magician, a Jewish false prophet whose name was Bar-Jesus, who was with the proconsul, Sergius Paulus, a man of intelligence. This man summoned Barnabas and Saul and sought to hear the word of God. But Elymas the magician (for thus his name is translated) was opposing them, seeking to turn the proconsul away from the faith. But Saul, who was also known as Paul, filled with the Holy Spirit, fixed his gaze on him, and said, "You who are full of all deceit and fraud, you son of the devil, you enemy of all righteousness, will you not cease to make crooked the straight ways of the Lord? And now, behold, the hand of the Lord is

upon you, and you will be blind and not see the sun for a time." And immediately a mist and a darkness fell upon him, and he went about seeking those who would lead him by the hand. THEN THE PROCONSUL BELIEVED WHEN HE SAW WHAT HAD HAPPENED, BEING AMAZED AT THE TEACHING OF THE LORD.

Acts 13:6-12

Paul did not work this act of power through some charisma of his own. He was filled with the Holy Spirit, even as Jesus had been. It is interesting that the proconsul turned his heart to Jesus based upon *"the teaching of the Lord,"* which was the work of God's justice against Satan's vessel Elymas. But now let us return to the life of Jesus for a moment.

After three years of service, the cross was before Him. This was the instrument of God's justice to utterly strip Satan of his authority and power. The work of Jesus on the cross completely divested Satan of his ability to hold mankind captive in the bondage of sin, that prison that kept man from a personal relationship with God.

When Jesus rose from the dead, He appeared to His disciples and gave them very specific instructions. He wanted them to follow His pattern in the proclamation of the Gospel.

...and He said to them, "Thus it is written, that the Christ should suffer and rise again from the dead the third day; and that repentance for forgiveness of sins should be proclaimed in His name to all the nations, beginning from Jerusalem. You are witnesses of these things. And behold,

Promised Joy, Promised Judgment

I am sending forth the promise of My Father upon you; but you are to stay in the city until you are clothed with power from on high."
Luke 24:46-49

These eleven men were witnesses to the death and resurrection of Jesus Christ. Pretty spectacular, right? But that witness was not enough to bring about a world change. That witness of itself would be by soulish power with human motivation—a witness that might last only as long as they themselves lived. Jesus said in this passage, "*You are witnesses of these things.*" But they were not His witnesses…not just yet. They needed a deposit from Him to change them from being just witnesses to being *His* witnesses. And they were to wait in the city for that impartation from God. The Holy Spirit whom the Man Jesus needed to establish the justice of God with authority and power was the same Holy Spirit who would now be needed by His disciples and followers.

…but you shall receive power when the Holy Spirit has come upon you; and you shall be My witnesses both in Jerusalem, and in all Judea and Samaria, and even to the remotest part of the earth.
Acts 1:8

The receiving of power through the impartation of the Holy Spirit from the throne of God was what these followers of Jesus needed! This is what would change them from merely being witnesses to being *Jesus'* witnesses. The Jesus who imparts the Holy Spirit is not only the Jesus who has been emptied to take on the form of a Man, but also the One who has conquered sin and death and is now seated on the highest throne in all creation. It is He who has received *all* authority and power in Heaven and earth (see Matthew 28:18). The Holy Spirit poured out is God's enforcement of the unmitigated, absolute justice won at the cross. The continued spread of the Gospel throughout the earth only comes by the work of the Holy Spirit in and through believers, not by charisma nor by human will.

Our foundation for the establishment of God's Kingdom and justice through our lives to the nations must only be this: *Jesus is the pattern.* However He accomplished this while He walked on earth is the only way we can do it. Jesus' walk here, through the testimony of the gospels, is the blueprint by which we will complete the commission to identically, successfully, and in even greater measure (see John 14:12) take this Gospel to the lost. Therefore, let us look at two key statements made by Jesus, for they show the foundation for His service in establishing the Kingdom of God on earth.

> *Jesus therefore answered and was saying to them, "Truly, truly, I say to you, the Son can do nothing of Himself, unless it is something He sees the Father doing; for whatever the Father does, these things the Son also does in like manner."*
> John 5:19

> *"For I did not speak on My own initiative, but the Father Himself who sent Me has given Me a commandment, to what to say and what to speak."*
> John 12:49

Jesus was *led by the Spirit* of His Father in everything

Promised Joy, Promised Judgment

He said and did. And that, beloved, is THE PATTERN! In this is relationship with our God and Father. Jesus taught His disciples that they would receive the same Holy Spirit He had and would be taught and led by Him (see John 14:26, 15:26-27, 16:13). After Jesus rose from the dead, He told His followers that, although they had been witnesses to His death and resurrection, they were to stay in the city until they had received from Heaven the promise of His Father. This was the same promise that He Himself had received at the commencement of His witness to the world. Thus, when the disciples were to receive the Holy Spirit, they would *say* and *do* by the leading of the Holy Spirit—just like Jesus. This is how they would proclaim, establish and enforce the justice of God in the nations to which they would go.

> *"But I tell you the truth, it is to your advantage that I go away; for if I do not go away, the Helper will not come to you; but if I go, I will send Him to you. And He, when He comes, will convict the world concerning sin, and righteousness, and judgment; concerning sin, because they do not believe in Me; and concerning righteousness, because I go to the Father, and you no longer behold Me; and concerning judgment, because the ruler of this world has been judged."* John 16:7-11

Jesus promised that the Holy Spirit, who was with His disciples, would actually come to dwell *within* them (see John 14:17). When the Holy Spirit was to take up residence in them, then He would "*convict the world concerning sin, and righteousness, and judgment.*" The Holy Spirit in us, working through us, does His work to convict the world. It is not our effort that convicts the world, but the Holy Spirit in and through us who convicts of sin and righteousness and judgment. This may seem overly simplistic. However, I believe we are too often caught up in trying to do the work of the Holy Spirit, desperately trying to convict people of sin ourselves. And that can lead to a lowering of the standards of the Gospel just to see the lost get "saved" so that we can point to our accomplishments in the Kingdom.

I do not imply that we ought not to be passionate in our proclamation of the Gospel, or that we cannot have a heart for the salvation of the lost. To the contrary, we need more of a heart for the lost in the Church today! But there must be a pure work of the Holy Spirit through our preaching in which *He* pricks the consciences of the hearers so that they know deep in their hearts that they are lost (see Acts 2, especially verse 37). Jesus often watched people walk away instead of repenting; yet He did not run after them to try to convince them to come to a lower standard. He knew they had to either repent by the conviction of the Holy Spirit or reject that conviction of sin (see Mark 10:17-22, John 6:52-67).

Those who responded to the Holy Spirit's conviction through the words and signs of Jesus received joy and a life of hope (see Luke 19:1-10). As they believed in Jesus and received the Holy Spirit, they were able to live before God in humility, purity and love for the Lord Jesus. Then they were used by the Holy Spirit to forward the good news of Kingdom justice to see the lost around them also respond to the mercy of God. (As an example, we can read the account of one such man in Acts 9:5-8.)

However, for those who reject God's mercy through the conviction of the Holy Spirit when they hear and see the preaching and demonstration of the Gospel, there is coming a Judgment Day in which they will have to give an account to the Judge.

Submitting to the justice of God in this life procures mercy in which future divine wrath will not be able to touch us. Rejecting the justice of God in this life provokes a judgment in which future mercy does not exist. It is the active work of the Holy Spirit now, in and through the believer, to offer the sinner forgiveness so that he will not have to stand in the defendant's box on Judgment Day.

Sixteen

Distributing Plunder: Evidence of God's Justice and Judgment

"...but when someone stronger than he attacks him and overpowers him, he takes away from him all his armor on which he had relied, and distributes his plunder." Luke 11:22

...and He will divide the booty with the strong; because He poured out Himself to death...
Isaiah 53:12a

The day Jesus was tried and crucified on that hill outside of Jerusalem was, to the natural eye, a day of defeat. The twelve chosen men were now eleven, one having hanged himself. These frightened men were scattered and in hiding. And although Satan thought it was a day for celebration, something had taken place that he was not quite able to put a finger on. The hour of darkness, he thought, was his hour of victory. But something on that hill of death had caused this evil leader to feel...stripped.

The sting of death had always been his crowning glory in the life of every human being...until this Man died. Somehow this evil leader just couldn't quite gloat. Something was wrong somewhere. It had seemed as though he had really had no control in even the dying breath of this Man. Satan's control over this one last moment in every man's life was not present with this particular Man.

Or had it been present—but then snatched away?

For three days Satan would know nothing of the fullness of his defeat at Calvary.

On the first day of the following week, the morning star introduced the dawn of a new day, and of a new era. It was time for the earthly reign of the new Kingdom. The Son of God did not wait for creation's sun to break over the horizon. Jesus burst forth from the tomb brighter than the first rays of our sun could ever shine. Victory glowed and shouted from the tomb. The angel pushed the stone away, introducing to this finite creation the physical Man who had defeated her enemy. The very enemy who had gripped creation since the first Adam gave in to the lie of the serpent generations before was now defeated!

In fifty days, a little more than a week after Jesus was caught up in the clouds on His way to the right hand of God in Heaven, He would begin to divide the booty of that plunder with 120 people (see Acts 2:4). These would take more and more plunder and share it with 3000 (see Acts 2:41), then 5,000 (see Acts 4:4)...and on...and on.

The treasures of Satan are the souls of mankind in every era and from every nationality. His only goal is to steal, kill and destroy people's lives until finally they perish forever without God.

> *Sheol and Abaddon are never satisfied....*
> Proverbs 27:20a

The plunder and booty taken by Jesus are those very souls—men, women and children—accumulated from all generations from the cities and countries of this world, from every tribe and every tongue. The Bible says that the earth is the Lord's, not the devil's (see Psalm 24:1). The blood of Jesus on the mercy seat in Heaven cries for mercy for those who dwell on God's earth. God is not idly sitting by, letting the blood of Jesus vainly cry out for mercy. Rather, He is actively taking back individuals, cities and nations from the clutches of Satan and his conniving, deceiving schemes.

As we have seen, the justice of God has authority and power to carry out God's verdict. The judgment of God against sin has been met by Jesus at the cross. Now is the time to proclaim liberty to all souls from the condemnation of sin that no longer has the right, authority or power to hold mankind in bondage. Now is the time to become an heir with Jesus in His plunder of Satan's strongholds. The nations of peoples belong to the Lord.

> *"I will surely tell of the decree of the* Lord: *He said to Me, 'Thou art My Son, today I have begotten Thee. Ask of Me, and I will surely give the nations as Thine inheritance, and the very ends of the earth as Thy possession.'"* Psalm 2:7-8

Promised Joy, Promised Judgment

> *"...for Thou wast slain, and didst purchase for God with Thy blood men from every tribe and tongue and people and nation."*
> Revelation 5:9b

Jesus was declared the Son of God with power through His resurrection from the dead (see Romans 1:4). He ascended to the throne of God and sat down as King over every authority and power on earth. The decree of the God of the universe is that every nation become the inheritance of Jesus, who purchased them with His blood!

But how does He take the cities and the nations if He has sat down in Heaven? How does Jesus get the very ends of the earth as His possession, His plunder? He gains them through those who are joint heirs with Him.

> *...but you have received a spirit of adoption as sons by which we cry out, "Abba! Father!" The Spirit Himself bears witness with our spirit that we are children of God, and if children, heirs also, heirs of God and fellow heirs with Christ...*
> Romans 8:15b-17a

We, beloved, are joint heirs with Jesus Christ in His inheritance. The prophet Isaiah said that *"He will divide the booty with the strong"* (Isaiah 23:12). We become strong, not by the might of our own strength, but by faith through the empowering of the Holy Spirit. That empowering enables us to take the plunder of the ends of the earth.

> *Thy people will volunteer freely in the day of Thy power...*
> Psalm 110:3a

Distributing Plunder: Evidence of God's Justice and Judgment

> *"...but you shall receive power when the Holy Spirit has come upon you; and you shall be My witnesses both in Jerusalem, and in all Judea and Samaria, and even to the remotest part of the earth."* Acts 1:8

When we are baptized, that is, immersed, in the Holy Spirit who was poured out from the throne of justice and judgment, we are volunteering to be Jesus' witnesses. Then we receive an impartation of divine power in order to partake with Jesus in seeing people freed from sin and won to the Kingdom of God. Remember, it is the Holy Spirit in us who convicts the world of sin, of righteousness and of judgment. We become joint heirs with Jesus, as the Holy Spirit works through the Gospel we proclaim, in taking the cities of this earth as an inheritance.

> *And when the day of Pentecost had come, they were all together in one place. And suddenly there came from heaven a noise like a violent, rushing wind, and it filled the whole house where they were sitting. And there appeared to them tongues as of fire distributing themselves, and they rested on each one of them. And they were all filled with the Holy Spirit and began to speak with other tongues, as the Spirit was giving them utterance.* Acts 2:1-4

There were Jews from all over the known world in Jerusalem at that time; they had gathered there for the Feast of Pentecost, an annual Jewish holiday celebrating the beginning of the harvest season. The foreign-

Promised Joy, Promised Judgment

born Jews heard the noise of the rushing wind and dashed over to the place where it had occurred. Upon arriving, they heard the 120 believers speaking in various tongues; that is, they were talking in specific languages native to those at the festival who had gathered from other countries.

What amazed the crowd was that the 120 believers speaking their languages were Galileans who had not learned these languages through natural means. Moreover, these Galileans were telling of the mighty deeds of God. The foreigners were quite perplexed, but their hearts were being stirred by the Holy Spirit because of the message of the Gospel. Listen to these foreign visitors voice their perplexity:

> *"And how is it that we each hear them in our own language to which we were born? Parthians and Medes and Elamites, and residents of Mesopotamia, Judea and Cappadocia, Pontus and Asia, Phrygia and Pamphylia, Egypt and the districts of Libya around Cyrene, and visitors from Rome, both Jews and proslytes, Cretans and Arabs—we hear them in our own tongues speaking of the mighty deeds of God." And they continued in amazement and great perplexity, saying to one another, "What does this mean?"* Acts 2:8-12

At this point, Peter, one of the eleven apostles and one of the 120 who had just received the Holy Spirit, stood up to give an answer to the question *"What does this mean?"* He preached to them the message of the cross and of the resurrection of Jesus Christ, and of their need to repent of sin.

Distributing Plunder: Evidence of God's Justice and Judgment

This whole scene took place because the 120 believers were volunteers in the day of God's power, that day being the Feast of Pentecost, which was the feast of first harvest. That day in Acts 2 was indeed the beginning of the harvest of nations, the beginning of Jesus distributing plunder of His own. That day, several thousand Jews and proselytes, the majority of whom had grown up in other than Israel, from present-day Italy to the borders of India, northern Africa, present-day Turkey and parts of southern Europe, submitted their hearts to Jesus. They were convicted by the Holy Spirit of sin and called to righteousness and judgment while listening to the Gospel message. Look at the power of the Holy Spirit working through Peter:

> *Now when they heard this, they were pierced to the heart, and said to Peter and the rest of the apostles, "Brethren, what shall we do?" And Peter said to them, "Repent, and each of you be baptized in the name of Jesus Christ for the forgiveness of your sins; and you shall receive the gift of the Holy Spirit. For the promise is for you and your children, and for all who are far off, as many as the Lord our God shall call to Himself." And with many other words he solemnly testified and kept on exhorting them, saying, "Be saved from this perverse generation!" So then, those who had received his word were baptized; and there were added that day about three thousand souls.*
>
> Acts 2:37-41

Some days later Peter and John were going to the Temple on a certain afternoon, as they were in the habit of doing. That day they came upon a man who needed healing, but who was begging for money. Being led by the Holy Spirit, Peter healed the man in Jesus' name (see Acts 3:1-4:31). This one act resulted in the plunder of five thousand people from Satan's domain. The evidence of God's justice by the work of Jesus' cross through Holy Spirit-baptized witnesses was shown before the eyes of all.

> *...and He will divide the booty with the strong; because He poured out Himself to death...*
> Isaiah 53:12

The work of Jesus' cross and His shed blood has not come to an end. The Holy Spirit who gives life and power through the message preached by volunteers in the day of His power is active to this day. It is the delight of God, not only to see souls brought into His Kingdom, but also to share the inheritance of cities and nations with His people.

Indeed, His heart in this was first evidenced in Abraham's day so many generations earlier. God Himself came to let Abraham know that a city was on the brink of doom, and to invite his intercession. God's heart was evidenced prophetically through Esther and Mordecai as different people groups turned to their God when His justice for Esther's people was shown to be stronger than the devil's plan of destruction. And in the book of Acts, the Holy Spirit bore witness to God's heart to share the inheritance as believers moved from city to city proclaiming the Gospel, and people turned their hearts to faith in Christ Jesus.

Our greatest joy is to personally be involved in proclaiming the Good News of Jesus, and then watching the Holy Spirit convict hearts to respond to that Good News. For it is here that you see the testimony of God's justice at work, as He makes you a joint heir in the plunder won by the *stronger* Man.

Seventeen

THE CITY OF TYRE: THE STANDARD ON JUDGMENT DAY!

If we were to document the revivals of history and write them in consecutive order, we would see that God has moved powerfully among men in what would appear to be spurts on a time line of slowly moving history. It is difficult, I think, for the Church today to see these moves as any more than just that—a move of God that took place at whatever time He determined was good for that era. It is even more difficult today, when God moves by His Spirit in a powerful way to draw men after Himself, to see the long-term purposes of God in His divine timetable. We crash, if you will, and often come to a halt in our pressing on in God when the revival seems to stop; then we return to our walk in God with perhaps a bit more energy for a season to work with God in discipling new believers.

But there is a purpose in God's heart for those times of renewal and revival. He has long-term goals, as the Bride of Christ is prepared more and more for her soon-coming Groom. It is imperative, more than can be stated in mere words on a page, that any church which experiences revival in any measure understand her accountability—that is, her responsibility—in the long-term purposes of God for such supernatural works among men.

This chapter contains the very sobering story of a city that took lightly the work of God in her midst. We are desperate for the justice of Heaven in our cities today, to fulfill the Great Commission to take a harvest of souls from the nations. But if we cry out to Jesus for a work of revival or whatever sort of outpouring of Heaven is needed for our city, we must seriously understand that He will not pour out of Himself merely so we may experience a spiritual high. We are involved as joint heirs with Jesus in taking a Bride for Him from the cities and nations of the earth. We are involved in eternal, not temporal, actions, which will affect forever the lives of those among whom we dwell.

Let us look, then, at the account of this city.

There existed a city of antiquity by Israel on the east coast of the Mediterranean, about forty miles northwest of the Sea of Galilee. Known in history for its great wealth, its strong fortification, and its pride in both of these, the city entertained a false sense of invincibility and longevity. If you were to look at maps that depict the earliest of times in the land of Canaan, you would find this city. Its professionals were known throughout many nations in their part of the world for their skills in carpentry, masonry and bronze work, as well as being some of the best sailors on the seas. They were also skilled in making a dye for coloring cloth, a substance they were able to extract from some of the sea mussels and whelks. The cloth they were able to dye from this substance brought great wealth to that industry for this city, because the dye was so rare. In the natural, everything about this city of old spoke of excellence. This in turn became for them abundance; unfortunately, because of pride, it also produced arrogance.

The city of Tyre is so named for the double rock on which it was built; it had formerly been an island about a third of a mile off the mainland. The people of Tyre erected a wall around the very edge of the rock on which the city was built, rendering Tyre virtually impregnable. This proved invaluable throughout the years of her existence, as mighty kings of ancient days — Shalmaneser and Sennacherib of Assyria, and Nebuchadnezzar, the most famous and mighty of the kings of Babylon — were all unable to destroy or even penetrate Tyre, though they tried with great sieges.

Listen to some of the words of God through the Old Testament prophet Ezekiel concerning the splendor of this gem of antiquity:

> *Thus says the Lord GOD, "O Tyre, you have said, 'I am perfect in beauty.' Your borders are in the heart of the seas; your builders have perfected your beauty. They have made all your planks of fir trees from Senir; they have taken a cedar from Lebanon to make a mast for you. Of oaks from Bashan they have made your oars; with ivory they have inlaid your deck of boxwood from the coastlands of Cyprus. Your sail was of fine embroidered linen from Egypt so that it became your distinguishing mark; your awning was blue and purple from the coastlands of Elishah."*
>
> Ezekiel 27:3b-7

Promised Joy, Promised Judgment

The prophet continues to describe how inhabitants of the nations came to serve Tyre and to enhance her beauty and her activities. The Lord speaks of the ships of the nations that came to do business with the city; He speaks of her army and her might. The passage continues to describe the vast diversity of the commerce of Tyre:

> *"Tarshish was your customer because of the abundance of all kinds of wealth; with silver, iron, tin, and lead, they paid for your wares. Javan, Tubal, and Meshech, they were your traders; with the lives of men and vessels of bronze they paid for your merchandise. Those from Beth-togarmah gave horses and war horses and mules for your wares. The sons of Dedan were your traders. Many coastlands were your market; ivory tusks and ebony they brought as your payment. Aram was your customer because of the abundance of your goods; they paid for your wares with emeralds, purple, embroidered work, fine linen, coral, and rubies. Judah and the land of Israel, they were your traders; with the wheat of Minnith, cakes, honey, oil, and balm they paid for your merchandise. Damascus was your customer because of the abundance of your goods, because of the abundance of all kinds of wealth, because of the wine of Helbon and white wool. Vedan and Javan paid for your wares from Uzal; wrought iron, cassia, and sweet cane were among your merchandise. Dedan traded with you in saddlecloths for riding. Arabia and all the princes of Kedar, they were your customers for lambs,*

rams, and goats; for these they were your customers. The traders of Sheba and Raamah, they traded with you; they paid for your wares with the best of all kinds of spices, and with all kinds of precious stones, and gold. Haran, Canneh, Eden, the traders of Sheba, Asshur, and Chilmad traded with you. They traded with you in choice garments, in clothes of blue and embroidered work, and in carpets of many colors, and tightly wound cords, which were among your merchandise. The ships of Tarshish were the carriers for your merchandise. AND YOU WERE FILLED AND WERE VERY GLORIOUS in the heart of the seas."
                                                  Ezekiel 27:12-25

God took two dozen verses in His Book to describe the magnificence and the riches of this one city—and it wasn't even a city of His people Israel. Every imaginable sort of merchandise came to or was sold from this city. Tyre commanded the respect and wealth of the most significant, as well as the insignificant, cities of the known world. The famous city of Carthage was founded by the people of Tyre, as well as several other lesser known cities. So knowledgeable and skilled were this city's craftsmen that King Solomon of Israel, who had built the glorious and majestic Temple to God in Jerusalem, used the men of Tyre specifically to help with certain aspects of the Temple's construction, as well as with the artwork of the gold and bronze used in the Temple (see 1 Kings 5; 2 Chronicles 2:11-16).

Tyre was well known for her citizens' abilities in the expression of every possible creative talent. There may never have been a city since that has possessed such a wealth of knowledge and wisdom. The city became what it was because of the knowledge of her leader.

Look again at the words of God concerning this man:

> *The word of the LORD came again to me saying, "Son of man, say to the leader of Tyre, 'Thus says the Lord GOD, "Because your heart is lifted up and you have said, 'I am a god, I sit in the seat of gods, in the heart of the seas'; yet you are a man and not God, although you make your heart like the heart of God—behold, you are wiser than Daniel; there is no secret that is a match for you. By your wisdom and understanding you have acquired riches for yourself, and have acquired gold and silver for your treasuries. By your great wisdom, by your trade you have increased your riches, and your heart is lifted up because of your riches…'"* Ezekiel 28:1-5

When we read this, we have to stand back and marvel. What could this city have looked like? What kind of universities and medical facilities existed here? They seem to have had the ability to meet every material, medical and mental need possible in that day. In one city! What an astounding place. Every magazine and newspaper today would hold up Tyre as the city to model. And all other cities would envy the abundance of this one city.

But was Tyre the *supreme* model city?

This city's leader had one fundamental flaw, a defect that was reproduced in the people, an imperfection that would cause them to bear the fruit of that flaw. He forgot the divinity of his Creator, and the honor due Him

THE CITY OF TYRE: THE STANDARD ON JUDGMENT DAY!

alone. He forgot that Tyre's beauty and wisdom were not of herself, but given by God.

Because this was not addressed or corrected, the fruit of imperfection, which is corruption, began to show in all that Tyre did in her activity.

> *"You were blameless in your ways from the day you were created, until unrighteousness was found in you. By the abundance of your trade you were internally filled with violence, and you sinned.... Your heart was lifted up because of your beauty; you corrupted your wisdom by reason of your splendor. ...By the multitude of your iniquities, in the unrighteousness of your trade, you profaned your sanctuaries."*
>
> Ezekiel 28:15-18a

The ultimate city was not so ultimate in her business dealings or in the care and protection of her own people. The "survival of the fittest or the most cunning" became the rule. The wealthiest cared little for the poor. Merchants cheated each other or their customers wherever possible. Even their worship was corrupted. Morality was not an issue in this city that loved wealth and wisdom and might as her gods. The pride in this city's leader, and then in her people, brought the promise of eventual complete and utter destruction.

> *"...therefore, thus says the Lord GOD, 'Behold, I am against you, O Tyre, and I will bring up many nations against you, as the sea brings up its waves. And they will destroy the walls of Tyre and break down her towers; and I will scrape her de-*

bris from her and make her a bare rock. She will be a place for the spreading of nets in the midst of the sea, for I have spoken,' declares the Lord GOD, 'and she will become spoil for the nations.'"
Ezekiel 26:3-5

" 'Therefore, behold, I will bring strangers upon you, the most ruthless of the nations. And they will draw their swords against the beauty of your wisdom and defile your splendor. They will bring you down to the pit, and you will die the death of those who are slain in the heart of the seas. Will you still say, "I am a god," in the presence of your slayer, although you are a man and not God, in the hands of those who wound you? You will die the death of the uncircumcised by the hand of strangers, for I have spoken!' declares the Lord GOD!"
Ezekiel 28:7-10

Nebuchadnezzar, as previously mentioned, was one of the *"strangers"* and *"most ruthless of nations"* that would come upon Tyre in accordance with this prophetic word through Ezekiel. Nebuchadnezzar laid siege for thirteen years against this city in the water, and killed those on the mainland who were its citizens. But he could not destroy Tyre itself, although she did submit to the rulership of Babylon.

Tyre did not meet the most ruthless of nations and strangers until Alexander the Great came down the Mediterranean coastline from Macedonia. When this young Greek leader arrived at the water's edge and looked over to the city built on the rock several hun-

THE CITY OF TYRE: THE STANDARD ON JUDGMENT DAY!

dred yards out, he jumped at this challenge to his desire to conquer and rule. Thus began his attempt at conquest to bring down this great and magnificent city of antiquity. And proud Tyre mocked Alexander and his army relentlessly.

But Tyre did not know the character of this ruthless little man, hungry for conquest.

Alexander had his engineers build a mole, that is, a land bridge, from the mainland to the island city. Tyre's men responded by attacking his builders from their fortified wall towers…until Alexander duplicated those towers on the mole that was slowly inching toward Tyre. The Sidonians, Tyre's closest northern neighbors and her former allies, were the most recent of Alexander's conquests. Alexander had the men of Sidon build warships for his army, so they could protect his own engineers until they could complete the mole. The Greek leader was outraged at the scoffing and rebellion of this once impregnable city. When he finally penetrated Tyre's walls, he shed much blood and then razed the city down to the rock, throwing the pillars and wall into the sea…exactly as God had spoken through His prophet several hundred years before.

According to the history books and encyclopedias, today the bare rock, which was once the foundation stone for Tyre, is used by fishermen for drying their nets. (See Ezekiel 26:14.) Tyre's judgment was decidedly final:

> *"Then I shall bring you down with those who go down to the pit, to the people of old, and I shall make you dwell in the lower parts of the earth,*

Promised Joy, Promised Judgment

like the ancient waste places, with those who go down to the pit, so that you will not be inhabited; but I shall set glory in the land of the living.
Ezekiel 26:20

The story and, yes, even the bare rock today are warnings against cities who would fill themselves with contempt and pride, being puffed up by their earthly knowledge and industry, neglecting others and forgetting God.

But that is *not* the point of this writing!

There is something even more sobering about this story for cities that have experienced the mighty work of God through revival. This city of Tyre, like the city of Sodom, discussed earlier in this book, was wicked to the core. However, like Sodom, Tyre will have a position with God on the last day of this age that will jolt the most humble of saints and will horrify those who think their religiosity has any bearing with the Almighty.

We must look at a New Testament city to understand the difference between wicked Tyre and the "better" cities. Then we will look at Tyre's and Sodom's standing before the Judge of all.

Perhaps the most direct line of travel from Tyre to the north end of the Sea of Galilee brings us to the very few remaining ruins of the New Testament city of Capernaum. It was situated at the northwest corner of the Sea of Galilee, and was in the territory of Galilee. Galilee was the region that was home to Jesus, both as He grew up in Nazareth and during many days of His ministry. The people of Galilee, as well as of Decapolis and Phoenicia, regions southeast and northwest of the sea, accepted Him, whereas Judea's religious community constantly rejected and persecuted Him.

The City of Tyre: The Standard on Judgment Day!

And leaving Nazareth, He came and settled in Capernaum, which is by the sea.
Matthew 4:13

When therefore the Lord knew that the Pharisees had heard that Jesus was making and baptizing more disciples than John,…He left Judea, and departed again into Galilee. … For Jesus Himself testified that a prophet has no honor in his own country.
John 4:1-3, 44

Thus the Son of God, with miracles and signs and wonders, was doing more of the work of Heaven in Capernaum, as well as in Bethsaida and Chorazin, two towns also located on the north end of the Sea of Galilee, than in Judea. The towns and cities of Judea did not see the numbers of miracles that these three cities did. How awesome, how wonderful, to behold the Son of God, with a continuous flow of miracles! What more could Capernaum ask than to have God reveal His only begotten Son, with a flow of Heaven's power, in their city? The Lord Jesus even chose a few of His apostles from their region.

Look at just a few of the things accomplished in their locality:

And when He had entered Capernaum…. And when Jesus had come to Peter's home, He saw his mother-in-law lying sick in bed with a fever. And He touched her hand, and the fever left her; and she arose and waited on Him. And when evening had come, they brought to Him many who were demon-possessed; and He cast out the spirits with

Promised Joy, Promised Judgment

a word, and healed all who were ill in order that what was spoken through Isaiah the prophet might be fulfilled, saying, "HE HIMSELF TOOK OUR INFIRMITIES, AND CARRIED AWAY OUR DISEASES."

Matthew 8:5, 14-17

In one day alone, Jesus healed Peter's mother-in-law of a fever, cast out demons, and healed many townspeople. And He would do many more miracles there. Capernaum, along with the other two neighboring towns of the northern coast of the Sea of Galilee, would see more of God's power than any other region of Israel (see Matthew 11:20). Compared with Tyre, Sidon, Sodom, Gomorrah or Nineveh, the cities of Capernaum, Bethsaida and Chorazin seemed excellent places to live and raise a family. These latter three cities were never known for violence or perversion. Not only that, but the Son of God was often seen there!

However, something even worse than what was in Tyre and in Sodom was in their character.

Something was so terribly wrong. Perhaps the natural eye of man could not perceive it. But to the eyes of the Judge of the whole earth, the Father of the Son of God, something was so iniquitous that the three cities gained for themselves a worse pronouncement of judgment than either Tyre or Sodom did.

Pay heed to the words of Jesus:

Then He began to reproach the cities in which most of His miracles were done, BECAUSE THEY DID NOT REPENT. "Woe to you, Chorazin! Woe to you, Bethsaida! For if the miracles had occurred in Tyre and Sidon which occurred in you,

THE CITY OF TYRE: THE STANDARD ON JUDGMENT DAY!

they would have repented long ago in sackcloth and ashes. Nevertheless I say to you, IT SHALL BE MORE TOLERABLE FOR TYRE AND SIDON IN THE DAY OF JUDGMENT, THAN FOR YOU. And you, Capernaum, will not be exalted to heaven, will you? You shall descend to Hades; for if the miracles had occurred in Sodom which occurred in you, it would have remained to this day. Nevertheless I say to you that it shall be more tolerable for the land of Sodom in the day of judgment, than for you." Matthew 11:20-24

Do you recall Tyre's final judgment? It was to *"dwell in the lower parts of the earth"* (Ezekiel 26:20). Do you see Capernaum's doomed end? It is to *"descend to Hades"*...the same place as Tyre. Do you think that maybe the inhabitants of Tyre are cursing and railing at the inhabitants of Capernaum right now? Why? Because Capernaum had seen the Son of God, had witnessed *most* of His miracles, and had seen the signs and wonders...yet the people of Capernaum did not repent!

About the fourth century A.D. there was an earthquake on the north end of the Sea of Galilee. Bethsaida, Chorazin and Capernaum were all destroyed in the quake. Some fifteen hundred years later, in 1905, a few remaining ruins of Capernaum were discovered under much earth. A gentleman invested money in order to try to rebuild the ruined synagogue there, but he died shortly after reconstruction began.

The city of Capernaum had met up with the judgment of Jesus' words—*because she had steadfastly refused to bend her knees to the mercy and kindness of God abundantly poured out through the work of Jesus in her midst.*

Promised Joy, Promised Judgment

When the two cities of Tyre and Sodom stand before the throne of almighty God on that great Judgment Day at the end of this age, their eternal judgment will be most feared. But before they are forever cast into that damnation, the One who sits on the throne, judging all the nations of the earth which have existed throughout time, will call up three cities: Bethsaida, Chorazin and Capernaum. These will stand next to the inhabitants of Tyre and Sodom. He will then look over the history books of the two wicked cities and the three moderately good cities, to see how much of Heaven touched each of them, and how they responded. He will see that Sodom did indeed revile the two angels He had sent to them, as well as the single testimony of a foreigner named Lot. He will declare to Capernaum and Chorazin and Bethsaida that Sodom rejected this tiny reach of Heaven that tried to bring them repentance.

Then the Judge on the throne of Heaven will turn and read to Sodom and Tyre from the chronicles of the three cities standing beside them. He will read aloud from these books the accounts of how He had sent His only Son to the three seaside cities. He will read of miracles of healing and the casting out of demons, of people set free from the bondages of darkness. The Judge will read to Tyre and Sodom some of the actual testimonies of those who received a wonderful touch of Heaven in their personal lives. He will look over to the leader of Tyre and tell him that a greater Leader than he, with wisdom unsurpassed in the entire history of man, walked and taught among the people of the three cities.

Then, gazing upon the inhabitants of Capernaum, the hometown of His Son, the Almighty will, with tears

THE CITY OF TYRE: THE STANDARD ON JUDGMENT DAY!

and a quiet voice, tell the people of Sodom and Tyre that Bethsaida, Chorazin and, yes, Capernaum did *not* repent and turn to Immanuel, the "God with us" who walked among them. The Judge will glance over to the damned of the two ancient metropolises and see them weeping, almost uncontrollably because, after hearing what was taught and what was done for the three "good" cities, Tyre and Sodom will realize that they *would have repented* in sackcloth, covered themselves in ashes and humbled themselves before God—if only the same opportunity had been afforded them.

When the people of the Sea of Galilee's three northern cities look upon the wicked men of Sodom and Tyre, and see them weeping and wailing, only then will they realize their own stupidity in rejecting all that the Almighty gave to them…but it will be too late.

Are you listening?

Eighteen

The Judgment Seat of Christ

For we must all appear before the judgment seat of Christ, that each one may be recompensed for his deeds in the body, according to what he has done, whether good or bad. Therefore knowing the fear of the Lord, we persuade men....
2 Corinthians 5:10-11

We have seen how God has judged in the past. We have looked at the need to see Him operate now to bring about justice in the earth.

But there is a day that we have all heard about and we shudder to honestly take into consideration. It is a day on which each one of us will stand before the throne of our Creator, Redeemer and God to give an account for our deeds in this life. Yes, for those who have believed in the Lord Jesus through the work of His cross, there is a cleansing from sin, and an escape from God's wrath of eternal damnation. Still, we must stand before the Judge of all and account for our walk as believers. Knowing this instills some fear...and it should...but not a fear that causes us to run away in terror, although we know our lives are not without sin. Even John the apostle wrote that we are not without sin merely because we have believed (see 1 John 1:8). Rather, this is a healthy fear of God that keeps us coming *now*, in this life, before the throne of grace, *"...that we may receive mercy and may find grace to help in time of need"* (Hebrews 4:16).

The knowledge of this judgment day for believers is the focus of this chapter. In no way is it my intent to pour out condemnation. Indeed, I am extremely aware, and have been made even more so during the writing of this book, of my own inadequacies and pride and stumbling and unbelief. However, in reading through the entire New Testament, it is clear that the writers of these books themselves were continually motivated to live lives of uprightness, humility and every godly characteristic named, because of an awareness that they had to stand before the Judge on Judgment Day.

> *And if you address as Father the One who impartially judges according to each man's work, conduct yourselves in fear during the time of your stay upon earth; knowing that you were not redeemed with perishable things like silver or gold from your futile way of life inherited from your forefathers, but with precious blood, as of a lamb unblemished and spotless, the blood of Christ.*
> 1 Peter 1:17-19

The throne of God established for justice and judgment is a mercy seat (see Hebrews 4:16, 9:24-26, 10:19-22, 12:22-24), and will not cease to be so on Judgment

Day. However, the blood on that mercy seat from the sacrifice of Jesus testifies that sin has been dealt a death blow. Sin no longer has authority over those who have been washed by the blood. Therefore the testimony of that blood on the mercy seat must agree on Judgment Day with the results of that victory in our lives, if we submit to it now in this life.

The judgment seat of Christ, that eternal throne room, is a fearful place. It is utterly filled up with the complete, perfect attributes of a holy God. It is on this basis that judgment will be rendered. Yet, however holy, pure and far beyond anything we see in ourselves that throne room of God is, it is nonetheless accessible to us *now, in this life*. It is there that we may go to obtain everything we need in this life that pertains to godliness (see Titus 2:11-12). The throne room is the place where provision for such in our lives is given gladly and without cost, to anyone who would come for it and *with absolutely no condemnation at all* (see Isaiah 55).

The knowledge of our requirement to appear before the judgment seat of Christ produces a godly fear. But this knowledge also brings with it a motivational, eternal, investment quality; that is to say, there is something that we can give now, in this life, for our eternal benefit. And God longs for us to do so. Look again at the words of Paul:

> *For we must all appear before the judgment seat of Christ, that each one may be recompensed for his deeds in the body, according to what he has done, whether good or bad. Therefore knowing the fear of the Lord, we persuade men....*
> 2 Corinthians 5:10-11

Promised Joy, Promised Judgment

I cannot speak with knowledge of nations outside the U.S. and Canada, but at least here we seem to possess a common shortcoming of character: Long-term investments seem very foreign to our instant society. Rarely do we hear of those who invest for the long term without a goal of swift, short-term, gratifying profits. We have relatively brief histories in the two North American nations. We do not, on a national scale, seem to plan our investments so as to benefit a distant future. We even bear witness to this fact with a common bumper sticker: "I'm spending my kids' inheritance."

The reason I mention this mindset is that I have seen this tendency also in the North American Church. We don't seem to have an eternal investment vision. Yet Paul's words testify that indeed we are making eternal investments by the way we live now, by making investments good or bad. The Judge on that judgment seat is not waiting to show us every sin we have ever committed. As already stated, the blood is there *now* to keep us clean when we do fall.

Rather, Jesus, as our Judge, has rewards, returns on investments, if you will, based on our walk before Him. He sees how we walk according to the knowledge of His grace in this life. Rewards in this life are short-term. But investments through a walk of humility and holiness based on grace and mercy will reap benefits for endless time to come. This therefore becomes an incentive for us to live for Jesus now, in this life, instead of for ourselves. That is the life to which we died when we were born again and were baptized.

> *"Already he who reaps is receiving wages, and is gathering fruit for life eternal…"*
>
> John 4:36a

The very lives we live as believers, whether good or bad, is a sowing of the Gospel into the lives of those around us. If we choose to live according to the life of sin, from which the blood of Jesus cleansed us, then we will not reap eternal benefits (see 1 Corinthians 3:11-15). Sin's result is always death (see Romans 6:15-18). Eternity consists only of life. If we choose to live by the grace of God provided through the blood of Jesus, then the testimony of God will go forth from our lives as truth and we will reap wages, gathering fruit for eternal life. The ongoing knowledge that we must stand before Jesus as a Judge motivates us to live a life that will persuade even the lost, the unbelievers, toward salvation.

I must therefore admit to you that in this present hour in North America, especially in the United States, this knowledge of the judgment seat of Christ is very, very distant. There is very little reaping of fruit for eternal life, because there is very little of the fear of a holy and just God. We believe in the saving grace of Jesus provided at the cross, but we generally do not believe in a Judgment Day that requires us to account for our lives *as believers*. Our walk is generally very selfish, holding to much immorality and greed, and seeing almost no power in the Gospel for radically changed lives.

I say this with much dismay, because I really love these two nations in which I have lived. Some of you will most assuredly retort that you have seen the Gospel of Christ radically change lives. I know it does; I have seen it myself. But we cannot deny that the power of the Gospel is not at work as mightily as it ought to be, given the numbers of churches and media here. It disturbs me greatly that so many churches are having so small an impact within our cities today, considering how powerful the message of the Gospel really is.

I believe much of this stems from so little a realization of a Judgment Day awaiting believers. It seems that Paul's statement might be somewhat different if made by this generation at present: "*Therefore, not realizing that we have to give an account before the judgment seat of Christ, and so not knowing the fear of the Lord, we do not persuade men ….*"

I do not mean to offend. I groan within for my city. I talk with friends who live in different cities, and find that their cities are not so very different from mine; and I groan some more. I see the competition between churches, and I ache. I work with and talk with people who go to different churches, and their daily walk and talk has absolutely no fruit resembling that which would grow from the tree of life. Instead, many of them show forth lives that do not differ at all from the lives of those who do not claim a knowledge of Christ. This is not to imply that every believer is like this. But the truth of the Gospel's power to impact our society is simply not taking place as it ought.

Beloved, we cannot honestly believe that God is going to pour out judgments on the earth against wicked men, yet overlook selfishness and lack of holiness in the Body of Christ. Judgment absolutely must begin with the household of God. Yet more than this, a motivation to please Jesus is what ought to keep us in a lifestyle that would gladly testify to the work of His blood in our lives.

> *Beloved, now we are children of God, and it has not appeared as yet what we shall be. We know that, when He appears, we shall be like Him, be-*

cause we shall see Him just as He is. AND EVERY-ONE WHO HAS THIS HOPE FIXED ON HIM PURIFIES HIMSELF, JUST AS HE IS PURE.
1 John 3:2-3

If we long to see Him, possessing no guile in that desire, we will work to look like Him now, in this life, so as not to be ashamed when He appears with His reward in hand. A desire to please Him who cleansed us through His death on the cross needs to possess us.

Would we stand in eternity having nothing to show forth throughout the endless ages because we chose to live for ourselves now, in this vapor of a life?

Nineteen

The Final White Throne Judgment

> *...it is appointed for men to die once and after this comes judgment...*   Hebrews 9:27

No biblical study of judgment would be complete without at least touching on the subject of the Great White Throne Judgment, a doctrine that was taught by the apostles. This chapter differs from the previous one because it speaks of the day when the ultimate verdict against the serpent who first deceived man will be carried out. That will also be the day when those who chose not to follow Christ will find out their eternal judgment, whether there will be mercy in Heaven for them. The final judgment is a day every man, woman and child will have to face, from the first man created to the last person yet to be born.

This is a message that must be heard by believers and unbelievers alike. It is a subject currently taught but little; and where the message is heard, it is often brought with much condemnation. There is too often little hope, but rather much terror for the hearer.

Promised Joy, Promised Judgment

Having said this, I do not mean to downplay that day in order to soften the impact of it. I cannot say that all will go well with everyone. However, God did have the topic of the final Judgment Day inscribed so that we can know something of it. It will be a landmark day in this age because it will be the last day of this age, this creation. There are, therefore, things to be taken with absolute seriousness *now*, in this life, which will dictate those judgments that will befall us on that day.

John the apostle received a revelation while in exile on the island of Patmos. In this vision, he was shown the final Judgment Day. The people of the earth, from all times in our world's history, were standing before the Judge of all.

> *And I saw a great white throne and Him who sat upon it, from whose presence earth and heaven fled away, and no place was found for them. And I saw the dead, the great and the small, standing before the throne, and books were opened; and another book was opened, which is the book of life; and the dead were judged from the things which were written in the books, according to their deeds. And the sea gave up the dead which were in it, and death and Hades gave up the dead which were in them; and they were judged, every one of them according to their deeds. And death and Hades were thrown into the lake of fire. This is the second death, the lake of fire. And if anyone's name was not found written in the book of life, he was thrown into the lake of fire.*
>
> Revelation 20:11-15

Death and Hades will give up every dead person. None will be held back from that White Throne Judgment. In that day earthly status will have no bearing on who stands where. Position for each will be based upon how each person treated others.

> ...and the dead were judged from the things which were written in the books, according to their deeds. Revelation 20:12

This passage can easily cause us to come under a feeling of condemnation. But we need to remember that Jesus' blood saves us from the wrath of God, that is, from a sentence of eternal condemnation. The ultimate outcome of Jesus' death is that we receive salvation when we believe. That faith for salvation will come into complete fulfillment on the day our eyes behold of Him. Our confidence on that day in court is that when God looks upon us, He will recognize a daughter or a son, not a soul that chose not to spend eternity with Him.

Again, I do not belittle the seriousness of that day. There will be some who will precede us in that courtroom who will be carried away to a sentence of condemnation. Still, the seriousness of the blood of Jesus over us will be the joy in the eyes of the Judge, if we believed here on earth in Jesus Christ and what He did for us on the cross. Yes, we must answer for deeds done in the body, and no, we are not perfect in the body. But thanks be to God through our Lord Jesus for His grace and mercy! This does not excuse a life of walking in sin once we have been cleansed. Why resurrect that life to which we have died when we believed and were bap-

Promised Joy, Promised Judgment

tized? And if we do sin, we have an Advocate, a Lawyer, One who has carried our sin Himself in His own body. So when we confess our sin, He is *now*, in this life, faithful and just to forgive us and cleanse us of our sin. Thus the records in those books spoken of in Revelation 20 will not be kept full of records of our sins.

I know that to some readers, my writing in this chapter may seem too light, without sincerity, considering what a fateful day that will be for every created soul. But I tell you the truth, this was the most difficult chapter to write. I had to walk away from writing for some time because I could not write this chapter. I have studied and prayed, pondered and wrestled with condemnation, for it is a day known in fullness only to God. Still, He has not left us in the dark concerning that day. He has given us confidence by faith if we will walk in obedience to the truth He reveals to us by His grace and mercy.

I believe the Lord answered my months-long inquiry by showing me once again for whom the final judgment is intended. Remember, condemnation on that judgment day is intended for the devil and the angels that followed him (see 2 Peter 2:4, Jude 6). The Lord went on to show me that those who walk like the devil, doing his works, are those who will end up with that same judgment. All who do the deeds of darkness, whether subtly or blatantly, will be condemned (2 Peter 3:7). If your deeds are continually ungodly, you face a judgment day that will bring you a condemnation of eternal fire (see Revelation 20:15). If your deeds are continually ungodly, it is unlikely that you have ever truly been cleansed from your sin.

> *The one who says, "I have come to know Him," and does not keep His commandments, is a liar, and the truth is not in him...* 1 John 2:4

> *Everyone who PRACTICES sin also practices lawlessness; and sin is lawlessness. And you know that He appeared in order to take away sins; and in Him there is no sin. No one who abides in Him sins; NO ONE WHO SINS HAS SEEN HIM OR KNOWS HIM. Little children, let no one deceive you; the one who practices righteousness is righteous, just as He is righteous; the one who PRACTICES SIN is of the devil; for the devil has sinned from the beginning.* 1 John 3:4-8a

John is not saying that believers never sin. Rather, he is clearly making a distinction between those who practice sin and those who practice walking uprightly before God. You must not be deceived, dear reader. Going to church is not your ticket to Heaven.

Has the Holy Spirit convicted you of your sin? Have you repented, turning away from your sin by asking Jesus to forgive you and cleanse you? If these things are so, then your walk will not be as it was. You will no longer be continually walking in your fleshly lusts, in anger, in envy, because He really has cleansed you from such as these. And you are practicing righteousness! But if you do sin, and you realize it, confess it so that you no longer continually walk in that thing (see 1 John 1:9).

But what if you do go to church, or you think your life is all right because you are kind to others, but you really do not pursue a relationship with Jesus Monday through Saturday? Is a little anger all right for you? Maybe a little gossip, a bit of envy or covetousness don't seem so bad. Maybe you're just leading your own kind of life, trying not to break the laws, or at least, trying not to get caught. Perhaps you cannot honestly say that you know Jesus has ever pinpointed sin in your life.

It really doesn't matter if you are a good person. If you are one who believes "God loves me because He loves everybody, and He wouldn't send anyone to Hell," then you'll be in for quite a shock when you have to stand before Him on that day.

Beloved reader, it is better that you find this out now rather than later. It is better for you to find out right here that you have been deceived. God does indeed love everybody. But the manner in which you live your everyday life, not just your Sunday morning ritual, shows forth your love for Him. If you choose by your life, by your practice, not to love Him, you will not find an open door to eternal life with Him. Now is the time to find this out. Now is the time for you to learn the truth about the final Judgment Day, where each of us, individually, *will* stand to give an account of the deeds done during our life on earth.

Beloved, God is patient toward you now (see 2 Peter 3:9). As long as you are in the body, you have a chance to be cleansed from your sin and come into personal relationship with this awesome God through His Son Jesus, whom He sent to receive your condemnation. Every one of us, bad and good although not perfect, deserves eternal judgment because of our sin. But Jesus came here and died on the cross—not for Himself, but for you.

If the prospect of standing before God makes you realize that you are not presently in good standing with Him, now is the time to get right with Him (see Matthew 5:25-26). Now is the time to receive the mercy He has already provided as a just payment for your sins. Do not be deceived, beloved reader. *Your* goodness alone is not perfect, and thus it is not the key to open Heaven's door to you. Jesus is the *only* way in.

If you were aiming for a target, it wouldn't matter whether you missed it by a few millimeters or by a mile. *You still would have missed it!* Bow down on your knees right now, wherever you are as you read this book, and look up to Jesus, who took every wrong that you have ever done upon Himself on the cross. Cry out to Him out loud: "Lord Jesus, I know I am guilty enough to be condemned forever. But Jesus, You took my sin in Your body on the cross. You died for me, that I might live forever with You. I ask You for mercy, Jesus. I ask You to forgive me and to cleanse me from my sins, from my evil thoughts and my evil deeds."

If the Holy Spirit brings to your remembrance wrongs that you have done, speak them aloud to Him and ask Him to forgive you for those specific things. Do not stop until you know that you have spoken to Him all the things He is showing you.

"Lord Jesus, I thank You for Your blood that cleanses me from sin. Thank You so much for eternal life, that I might know You more. Thank You that I can stand before You and that I will not be condemned, because You took my condemnation, giving me righteousness and justice and life. Lord Jesus, I ask You to baptize me in Your Holy Spirit to help me walk in justice all the days of my life." Begin to thank Him aloud for His Holy Spirit. Thank Him for eternal life. If you need to stop here and just praise Him or talk to Him, that is more important than continuing on in this book. Take your time with Him.

You can know now, in this life, that you have eternal life, that you are not under a sentence of condemnation because you have passed out of death into life.

Whoever confesses that Jesus is the Son of God, God abides in him, and he in God. And we have come to know and have believed the love which God has for us. God is love, and the one who abides in love abides in God, and God abides in him. By this, love is perfected with us, that we may have confidence in the day of judgment; because as He is, so also are we in this world. There is no fear in love; but perfect love casts out fear, because fear involves punishment, and the one who fears is not perfected in love.

1 John 4:15-18

These things I have written to you who believe in the name of the Son of God, IN ORDER THAT YOU MAY KNOW THAT YOU HAVE ETERNAL LIFE. 1 John 5:13

We have confidence through Jesus that we will not be in fear on the Day of Judgment. When we know we have eternal life, we have passed out of a judgment of condemnation. Fear involves punishment. But punishment does not await you when once you have believed in Jesus through what He accomplished for you on the cross. *He* has borne your punishment. And that, beloved, has bearing on Judgment Day!

Here is one final thought concerning that White Throne judgment:

> *Now to Him who is able to keep you from stumbling, and to make you stand in the presence of His glory blameless with great joy, to the only God our Savior, through Jesus Christ our Lord, be glory, majesty, dominion and authority, before all time and now and forever. Amen.*
>
> Jude 24-25

Twenty

A Cry for the City

I wrote at the beginning of this book that the event which gave my wife and me a change of heart toward cities was the renewal that was poured out in 1994, which started in Toronto and spread southward to our city here in Texas. This writing was prompted by my job delivering phone books in a business district within our city that happens to be the center of the homosexual community here, close to the center of Dallas.

While I was in the midst of my writing, a scripture stood out in my mind continually from the New Testament concerning Abraham:

By faith Abraham, when he was called, obeyed by going out to a place which he was to receive for an inheritance; and he went out, not knowing where he was going. By faith he lived as an alien in the land of promise, as in a foreign land, dwelling in tents with Isaac and Jacob, fellow heirs of the same promise; FOR HE WAS LOOKING FOR THE CITY WHICH HAS FOUNDATIONS, WHOSE ARCHITECT AND BUILDER IS

Promised Joy, Promised Judgment

GOD. By faith even Sarah herself received ability to conceive, even beyond the proper time of life, since she considered Him faithful who had promised; therefore, also, there was born of one man, and him as good as dead at that, as many descendants AS THE STARS OF HEAVEN IN NUMBER, AND INNUMERABLE AS THE SAND WHICH IS BY THE SEASHORE.

All these died in faith, without receiving the promises, but having seen them and having welcomed them from a distance, and having confessed that they were strangers and exiles on the earth. For those who say such things make it clear that they are seeking a country of their own. And indeed if they had been thinking of that country from which they went out, they would have had opportunity to return. But as it is, they desire a better country, that is a heavenly one.

THEREFORE GOD IS NOT ASHAMED TO BE CALLED THEIR GOD; FOR HE HAS PREPARED A CITY FOR THEM. Hebrews 11:8-16

During his lifetime on earth, Abraham had risked his life to rescue the people of the wicked city of Sodom. Years later he stood in the gap in prayer for this wicked city, after God had told him that He was about to destroy it. The Holy Spirit spoke to me after I had finished writing about Abraham and Sodom. He brought to my remembrance this passage from Hebrews, specifically the verse saying that Abraham *"was looking for the city which has foundations, whose architect and builder is God."* The Holy Spirit said to me, *"THOSE WHO DO NOT LONG FOR THE CITY WHICH HAS FOUNDATIONS WILL NOT LONG FOR THE CITIES ON EARTH."*

You see, beloved, the city which has foundations, whose architect and builder is God is a city that will be made up of men and women, teenagers, boys and girls—people redeemed from broken-down, worldly, sinful, wicked cities of the earth.

> *"Cities of ruthless nations will revere Thee."*
> Isaiah 25:3b

The longing for that city designed and constructed by God will cause us to long for and participate in (whatever that level of participation may be) the salvation of the Sodoms and Tyres of this world.

Those who have their sights set on the city to come do not ignore the horror of eternal judgments that will befall the cities on earth. They know that the heavenly city has the foundation of a rejected Cornerstone; and they understand it was rejected as such for bearing the fullness of the sins of mankind so the cities of earth can be set free from the wickedness of sin and from eternal damnation. These who are the seed of Abraham and so intercede for wicked cities are marked on their foreheads (see Ezekiel 9:4) with a new name, an eternal name, which bears witness to the Lamb of God and to God Himself...and to that city which has foundations (see Revelation 3:12). And God is not ashamed to be called their God. For this God of justice so loved the world that He gave His only begotten Son, that whosoever, in whichever city of any and every nation, believes in Jesus, the Redeemer of cities, will have everlasting life in an eternal, just, love-packed city, which has the throne of their Redeemer right smack in the middle of that city.

Promised Joy, Promised Judgment

And I saw the holy city, new Jerusalem, coming down out of heaven from God.... And I heard a loud voice from the throne, saying, "Behold, the tabernacle of God is among men, and He shall dwell among them, and they shall be His people, and God Himself shall be among them, and He shall wipe away every tear from their eyes; and there shall no longer be any death; there shall no longer be any mourning, or crying, or pain; the first things have passed away." ...And he carried me away in the Spirit to a great and high mountain, and showed me the holy city, Jerusalem, coming down out of heaven from God, having the glory of God. Her brilliance was like a very costly stone, as a stone of crystal-clear jasper. It had a great and high wall, with twelve gates, and at the gates twelve angels; and names were written on them, which are those of the twelve tribes of the sons of Israel. Revelation 21:2-4, 10-12

And he showed me a river of the water of life, clear as crystal, coming from the throne of God and of the Lamb, in the middle of its street. And on either side of the river was the tree of life, bearing twelve kinds of fruit, yielding its fruit every month; and the leaves of the tree were for the healing of the nations. And there shall no longer be any curse; and the throne of God and of the Lamb shall be in it, and His bond-servants shall serve Him; and they shall see His face, and His name shall be on their foreheads.

Revelation 22:1-4